A NavPress Bible study on the book of

1 TIMOTHY

NAVPRESS
BRINGING TRUTH TO LIFE
NavPress Publishing Group
P.O. Box 35001, Colorado Springs, Colorado 80935

The Navigators is an international Christian organization. Our mission is to reach, disciple, and equip people to know Christ and to make Him known through successive generations. We envision multitudes of diverse people in the United States and every other nation who have a passionate love for Christ, live a lifestyle of sharing Christ's love, and multiply spiritual laborers among those without Christ.

NavPress is the publishing ministry of The Navigators. NavPress publications help believers learn biblical truth and apply what they learn to their lives and ministries. Our mission is to stimulate spiritual formation among our readers.

ISBN 08910-99530

Printed in the United States of America

1 2 3 4 5 6 7 8 9 10 11 12 13 14 15 / 99 98 97 96

CONTENTS

How to Use This Study   5
Background—The Epistle of 1 Timothy   11
    Map of the Roman Empire   11
    Outline of 1 Timothy   13
One—Overview (1:1-2)   15
Two—Beware of False Teachers (1:3-11)   25
Three—Grace! (1:12-17)   35
Four—How the Church Works (1:18–2:15)   45
Five   Officers in the Church (3:1-13)   57
Six—A Word to Timothy (3:14–4:16)   67
Seven—Various Instructions (5:1–6:2)   77
Eight—The Love of Money (6.3-10,17-19)   87
Nine—Final Charge (6:11-16,20-21)   95
Ten—Looking Back   103
Study Aids   107

ACKNOWLEDGMENTS

The LIFECHANGE series has been produced through the coordinated efforts of a team of Navigator Bible study developers and NavPress editorial staff, along with a nationwide network of fieldtesters.

AUTHOR: STEVE HALLIDAY
SERIES EDITOR: KAREN LEE-THORP

HOW TO USE THIS STUDY

This LIFECHANGE guide to the book of 1 Timothy is designed to give students a good overview of the first of what are known as the "pastoral epistles." While not everyone likes the designation "pastoral epistles,"[1] it has become the accepted term to describe three short letters (1 and 2 Timothy, and Titus) of instruction from the Apostle Paul to two young men who had been given great responsibility for the care of two local churches. Not only does 1 Timothy give explicit directions for basic church functions, but it also shows how an elder in the faith can instruct and motivate a younger believer to become a fine and able leader.

Objectives

Although the LIFECHANGE guides vary with the individual books they explore, they share some common goals:

1. To provide you with a firm foundation of understanding and a thirst to return to each book;
2. To teach you by example how to study a book of the Bible without structured guides;
3. To give you all the historical background, word definitions, and explanatory notes you need, so that your only other reference is the Bible;
4. To help you grasp the message of each book as a whole;
5. To teach you how to let God's Word transform you into Christ's image.

Each lesson in this study is designed to take 60 to 90 minutes to complete on your own. The guide is based on the assumption that you are completing one lesson per week, but if time is limited you can do half a lesson per week or whatever amount allows you to be thorough.

Flexibility

LIFECHANGE guides are flexible, allowing you to adjust the quantity and depth of your study to meet your individual needs. The guide offers many optional ques-

5

tions in addition to the regular numbered questions. The optional questions, which appear in the margins of the study pages, include the following:

Optional Application. Nearly all application questions are optional; we hope you will do as many as you can without overcommitting yourself.

For Thought and Discussion. Beginning Bible students should be able to handle these questions, but even advanced students need to think about them. These questions frequently deal with ethical issues and other biblical principles. They often offer cross-references to spark thought, but the references do not contain obvious answers. These questions are good for group discussions.

For Further Study. These questions include: (a) cross-references that shed light on a topic the book discusses, and (b) questions that delve deeper into the passage. You can omit them to shorten a lesson without missing a major point of the passage.

If you are meeting in a group, decide together which optional questions to prepare for each lesson and how much of the lesson you will cover at the next meeting. Normally, the group leader should make this decision, but you might let each member choose his or her own application questions.

Sometimes there is space in the margins of the study guide to jot answers to optional questions or notes from your discussion. However, you will often want more space for such notes. You can use the blank pages between lessons and at the end of the guide for notes, or you can begin a separate Bible study notebook. A separate notebook will give you plenty of room to answer optional questions, record prayer requests and answers to prayer, write notes from discussions, plan applications and record results, and describe experiences in your life that are teaching you spiritual lessons. A notebook like this can be invaluable.

As you grow in your walk with God, you will find the LIFECHANGE guide growing with you—a helpful reference on a topic, a continuing challenge for application, a source of questions for many levels of growth.

Overview and details

The study begins with an overview of 1 Timothy. The key to interpretation is context—what is the whole passage or book *about*? And the key to context is purpose—what is the author's *aim* for the whole work? In the first lesson you will lay the foundation for your study by asking yourself, "Why did the author (and God) write the book? What did he want to accomplish? What is the book about?"

Then over the next eight lessons, you will analyze successive passages in detail. You'll interpret particular verses in light of what the whole paragraph is about, and paragraphs in light of the whole passage. You'll consider how each passage contributes to the total message of the book. (Frequently reviewing an outline of the book will enable you to make these connections.) Then, once you understand what the passage says, you'll apply it to your own life.

In lesson 10, you will review Paul's major instructions to Timothy and review the whole epistle, returning to the big picture to see whether your view of it has changed after closer study. Review will also strengthen your grasp of major issues and give you an idea of how you have grown from your study.

Kinds of questions

Bible study on your own—without a structured guide—follows a progression. First you observe: What does the passage *say*? Then you interpret: What does the passage *mean*? Lastly you apply: How does this truth *affect* my life? The wording of a question in the guide nearly always makes an interpretation itself; so you may want to observe first *before* looking at the questions.

Some of the "how" and "why" questions will take some creative thinking, even prayer, to answer. Some are opinion questions without clear-cut right answers; these will lend themselves to discussions and side studies.

Don't let your study become an exercise of knowledge alone. Treat the passage as God's Word, and stay in dialogue with Him as you study. Pray, "Lord, what do You want me to see here?" "Father, why is this true?" "Lord, how does this apply to my life?"

It is important that you write down your answers. The act of writing clarifies your thinking and helps you remember what you have learned.

Study aids

A list of reference materials, including a few notes of explanation to help you make good use of them, begins on page 107. This guide is designed to include enough background to let you interpret with just your Bible and the guide. Still, if you want more information on a subject or want to study a book on your own, try the references listed.

Scripture versions

Unless otherwise indicated, the Bible quotations in this guide are from the *New International Version* of the Bible. Use any translation you like for study, preferably more than one. While a paraphrase such as *The Message* is not suitable for study, it can be helpful for comparison or devotional reading.

Memorizing and meditating

A psalmist wrote, "I have hidden your word in my heart that I might not sin against you" (Psalm 119:11). If you write down a verse or passage that challenges or encourages you, and reflect on it often for a week or more, you will find it beginning to affect your motives and actions. We forget quickly what we read once; we remember what we ponder.

When you find a significant verse or passage, copy it onto a card to keep with you. Set aside five minutes during each day just to think about what the passage might mean in your life. Recite it over to yourself, exploring its meaning. Then, return to the passage as often as you can during the day for a brief review. You will soon find it coming to mind spontaneously.

For group study

Why study in groups? Two reasons come immediately to mind: *accountability* and *support*. When each member commits to the others to seek growth in an area of life, you can pray with one another, listen jointly for God's guidance, help one another resist temptation, assure each other that the other's growth matters to you, use the group to practice spiritual principles, and so on. Pray about one another's commitments and needs at most meetings. Spend the first few minutes of each meeting sharing any results from applications prompted by previous lessons. Then discuss new applications toward the end of the meeting. Follow such sharing with prayer for these and other needs.

A group of four to ten people allows the richest discussions, but you can adapt this guide for groups of all sizes. It will suit a wide range of group types, such as home Bible studies, growth groups, youth groups, and business professionals' studies. Both new and experienced Bible students, and new and mature Christians will benefit from the guide. You can omit or leave for later any questions you find too easy or too hard.

This guide is designed to lead a group through one lesson per week, but feel free to split lessons if you want to discuss them more thoroughly. Or, omit some questions in a lesson if preparation or discussion time is limited. You can always return to this guide for personal study later on. You will be able to discuss only a few questions at length, so choose some for discussion and others for background. Make time at each meeting for members to ask about anything that gave them trouble.

Each member should prepare for the study by writing answers for all the background and discussion questions to be covered. If the group decides not to take an hour per week for private preparation, then expect to take at least two meetings per lesson to work through the questions. Application will be very difficult, however, without private thought and prayer.

If you write down each other's applications and prayer requests, you are more likely to remember to pray for them during the week, to ask about them at the next meeting, and to notice answered prayers. You might want to get a notebook for prayer requests and discussion notes.

Notes taken during discussion will help you remember, follow up on ideas, stay on the subject, and clarify a total view of an issue. But don't let note taking keep you from participating. Some groups choose one member at each meeting to take notes. Then someone copies the notes and distributes them at the next meeting. Share these tasks so that everyone will feel included and no one will feel burdened. Some groups have someone take notes on a large pad of paper or erasable marker board (preformed shower wallboard works well), so that everyone can see what has been recorded.

Structuring group time

The following structure suggests one possible way to organize your discussions; feel free to adapt these suggestions in whatever way best suits your group.

Worship. Some groups like to begin with prayer and/or singing. Some pray only briefly for God's guidance at the beginning and leave extended prayer time until after the study.

Warm up. Profitable studies lay a good foundation early on for honest sharing of ideas, for getting comfortable with each other, and for encouraging a sense of common purpose. One way to establish common ground is to talk about what each group member hopes to get out of your study and out of any prayer, singing, outreach, or anything else you might do together. You might also discuss what you hope to give to the group. If you have someone write down each member's hopes and expectations, you can look back at these goals later to see if they are being met. You can then plan more time for prayer or decide to move more deliberately through the study.

Take some time at the outset to talk about goals. Some groups use one session to hand out study guides, introduce the study, examine the "How to Use This Study" section on pages 5-10, and discuss goals.

First impressions. You may find it helpful to discuss each member's first impressions as you progress through the study. What was most helpful? Did anything startle you? What questions do you have? What overall impression did you gain from the session?

To focus your discussion, you might ask each group member to choose one scene or teaching that was especially meaningful to him or her, and explain why. This open sharing often helps members get better acquainted.

Study. Follow the study guidelines in whatever manner best helps you to grasp the meaning of the biblical text. It should be your overall goal to gain a thorough understanding of the passage under review.

Application. The last step of Bible study is asking yourself, "What difference should this passage make in my life? How should it make me want to think or act?" Application will require time, thought, prayer, and perhaps discussion with someone else.

At times, you may find it most productive to concentrate on one specific application, giving it careful thought and prayer. At other times you may want to list the implications a passage of Scripture has for your life, and then choose one to focus on for prayer and action. Use whatever method helps you grow more obedient to God's Word.

Some possible applications for a passage: "I need to ask God for the ability and discipline to obey by His Spirit." "I need to stop . . . " "I need to ask the Holy Spirit to help me . . ." "I believe I should. . . ."

As you develop applications, remember that we must cooperate with God if we are to grow spiritually; both we and God have a part to play (Philippians 2:12-13).[2] Effective applications must be saturated with prayer for guidance, ability, forgiveness, discipline, encouragement, and so on.

If application is unfamiliar to some group members, choose a sample paragraph from the epistle and discuss possible ways of applying it. Try to state specifically how the passage is relevant to you and how you might act in light of it. Think of responses that you might actually make, not merely ideal responses. Don't neglect prayer for ability, courage, discipline, and guidance to carry out the response you have identified!

Give the group a chance to voice any questions about the passages under review or historical/cultural references that may puzzle them. You may decide to postpone answering some questions until you have access to appropriate information. It's a good idea to keep a list of such questions and to ask a group member to look for more information and share the answer the next time you meet. (The Study Aids found on pages 107-111 offer ideas on where to begin looking for answers.)

Wrap-up. The wrap-up is a time to bring the discussion to a focused end and to make any announcements about the next lesson or meeting. Most of the lessons in this study cover more than one chapter of the epistle; your group may decide to tackle some of these lessons in more than one session. Make sure you decide ahead of time how much of each lesson you plan to study at your next meeting.

Worship. Praise God for His wisdom in giving us the teaching, principles, inspiration, and encouragement found in 1 Timothy. Praise Him for what He reveals about Himself in this book and ask Him to teach you to know, love, and obey Him throughout your study of 1 Timothy.

1. D. Edmond Hiebert, for example, prefers to use the term "Ecclesiological group" rather than "pastoral epistles" because "although the [latter] term is convenient, it is not altogether appropriate. It suits 1 Timothy and Titus quite well if the term is not used to misinterpret the position of these men [who, in Hiebert's view, were not pastors but special representatives of Paul]. It is much less suitable to 2 Timothy, which is quite largely personal. The epistles contain more than is implied in the term." D. Edmond Hiebert, *An Introduction to the New Testament: Volume Two, The Pauline Epistles* (Chicago: Moody Press, 1977), p. 307.
2. Jerry Bridges' book *The Discipline of Grace* (NavPress, 1995) examines the parts both we and God play in our spiritual growth.

BACKGROUND

The Epistle of 1 Timothy

Map of the Roman Empire

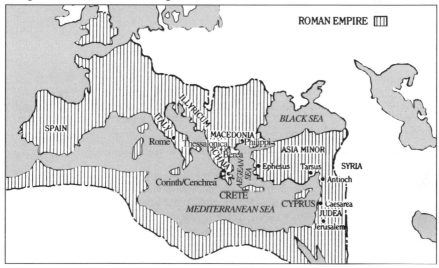

Since the early nineteenth century, the pastoral epistles—including 1 Timothy—have been more severely attacked than any of the other ten Pauline letters. Questions about their authorship and genuineness have raged since 1807 when Schleirmacher denied that Paul wrote them.[1]

Author

While traditional and conservative scholarship continues to hold that Paul did in fact pen these letters that bear his name, at least four arguments are commonly raised against that possibility:[2]

1. *Historical*

If Paul was put to death at the end of his Roman imprisonment described at the end of Acts, as many believe, then the events recorded in the pastoral epistles cannot be made to fit within the chronology of Acts. That means that Paul could not have written these epistles.

Yet if Paul was released from his Acts imprisonment and made additional journeys—as is most likely the case—then there is nothing to bar him from writing 1 Timothy before a second and final Roman imprisonment. Clement of Rome (A.D. 95) and the Muratorian Canon (c. A.D. 200) both say that Paul traveled to the extreme limit of the west, or Spain, a journey that is not recorded in Acts. And Eusebius (A.D. 326) says explicitly that Paul was taken prisoner in Rome a second time, where he wrote 2 Timothy and was then martyred.

2. *Ecclesiastical*

Some scholars claim that 1 Timothy displays a more advanced church organization than could have existed in the time of Paul. Yet when the pastorals are compared with the Epistles of Ignatius (c. A.D. 115), it becomes clear that the church organization in the former letters is far less developed than in the latter. Thus a second century date for the pastorals seems unlikely.

3. *Doctrinal*

Some authorities claim that the pastoral epistles focus on doctrinal problems which did not surface until after the death of Paul, citing especially the pastorals' emphasis on "sound doctrine" and their opposition to Gnostic ideas. Yet today it is conceded that Gnostic ideas had already invaded Judaism before Paul's day. (See the box, "Gnosticism" on page 25.)

4. *Linguistic*

The difference in style and vocabulary between the pastorals and Paul's other writings is regarded as the strongest argument against Pauline authorship. And it is true that a high percentage of the words used in the pastorals are not found elsewhere in Paul's writings. Yet it is highly probable that differences in subject matter, circumstances, and addressees can account adequately for the discrepancy. Some scholars have supposed that a secretary or scribe, perhaps Luke, was given a good deal of leeway in transcribing Paul's thoughts in these epistles. Whatever the case, there remain solid and good reasons to accept the traditional view that Paul was the author of 1 Timothy and the other two pastorals.

Date

Paul's first Roman imprisonment is usually dated anywhere from A.D. 59 to 64, while the early church without exception declares that Paul was executed by Emperor Nero (who died in June of A.D. 68). It is likely that Paul wrote 1 Timothy from Macedonia (1 Timothy 1:3), sometime between A.D. 64 and 66.[3]

Recipient

Timothy was a young man of mixed Jewish-Greek descent whom Paul probably met on his first missionary journey as recorded in Acts 13:4–14:27. While little is said of his Greek father, Timothy's Jewish mother and grandmother are both stated to be believers. Paul frequently referred to Timothy as his "son" (see Philippians 2:22; 1 Timothy 1:2,18; 2 Timothy 1:2; 2:1), which probably means either that he was won to Christ under the ministry of Paul (but see Acts 16:1) or that he was trained in the ministry under Paul. When the apostle saw that the young man had great promise for leadership, he had him circumcised and took him along as a younger associate.

Paul often sent Timothy on special assignments to difficult ministries — to Thessalonica (1 Thessalonians 3:1-10), to Corinth (1 Corinthians 4:17, 16:10-11), to Macedonia (Acts 19:22), to Philippi (Philippians 2:19-24), and to Ephesus (1 Timothy 1:3). While some have taken Paul's directives to Timothy as evidence that the young man was timid and diffident, it seems unlikely that Paul would have entrusted such difficult ministries to a man who lacked courage or decisiveness. It seems more likely that Paul's instructions are intended to encourage a young man who was facing intense opposition in Ephesus.

Background and purpose

The purpose of 1 Timothy seems clear from the third verse where Paul instructed his friend to "stay there in Ephesus so that you may command certain men not to teach false doctrines any longer." Paul clearly wrote 1 Timothy not only to counteract false teachings but also to encourage Timothy to stand for and proclaim the truth. The apostle also gives numerous instructions and advisories concerning various problems that either had or probably would arise in the church.

A strong Old Testament flavor fills the book. Note such phrases as "God our Savior" in 1:1 and 2:3 found nowhere else in Paul's writings. This is also the book where Jesus Christ is flatly stated to be our only "mediator between God and men" (1 Timothy 2:5) who gave himself as a "ransom" (2:6) for us.

Yet this book is not so much theological as it is *practical*. Timothy had already been instructed in the faith; what he needed in this difficult ministry was practical guidance on how to direct the affairs of the church in such a way that it would grow in the grace and knowledge of Jesus Christ. And that is just what we find in 1 Timothy.

Outline

A. Salutation (1:1-2)
B. Warning Against False Teachers (1:3-11)
    1. Warning against myths and endless genealogies (1:3-4)
    2. The goal of the command (1:5)

    3. False teachers (1:6-7)
    4. Purpose of the Law (1:8-11)
C. The Lord's Grace to Paul (1:12-17)
    1. Abundant grace (1:12-14)
    2. Unlimited patience (1:15-16)
    3. Doxology (1:17)
D. Paul's Charge to Timothy (1:18-20)
    1. Charge to fight the good fight (1:18-19a)
    2. Warning about shipwrecking the faith (1:19b-20)
E. Instructions for the Church (2:1–3:16)
    1. Instruction on prayer (2:1-4,8)
    2. Jesus the Mediator (2:5-6)
    3. Paul the apostle (2:7)
    4. Women in worship (2:9-15)
    5. Qualifications of overseers (3:1-7)
    6. Qualifications of deacons (3:8-13)
    7. Conclusion and doxology (3:14-16)
F. Instructions to Timothy (4:1–6:10,17-19)
    1. Warning against false teachings in later times (4:1-8)
    2. Hope in the living God (4:9-10)
    3. Instruction regarding church activities (4:11-16)
    4. Instruction regarding personal relationships (5:1-2)
    5. Instruction regarding widows (5:3-16)
    6. Instruction regarding elders (5:17-20)
    7. Charge to keep Paul's instructions (5:21)
    8. Instruction regarding purity (5:22)
    9. Instruction regarding personal health (5:23)
    10. Instruction regarding coming judgment (5:24)
    11. Instruction regarding slaves (6:1-2)
    12. Instruction regarding money (6:3-10)
    13. Instruction regarding the rich (6:17-19)
G. Paul's Final Charge to Timothy
    1. Charge to keep Paul's commands (6:11-15a)
    2. Doxology (6:15b-16)
    3. Final charge and warning (6:20-21)

1. D. Edmond Hiebert, *An Introduction to the New Testament: Volume Two, The Pauline Epistles* (Chicago: Moody Press, 1977), p. 308.
2. Frank E. Gaebelein, ed., *The Expositor's Bible Commentary: Volume 11*, Ralph Earle, "1 and 2 Timothy" (Grand Rapids: Zondervan Publishing House, 1978), pp. 341-343.
3. Thomas D. Lea, *The New American Commentary*, "1–2 Timothy, Titus" (Nashville: Broadman Press, 1992), p. 41.

LESSON ONE
1 TIMOTHY
1:1-2

Overview

The best way to introduce yourself to 1 Timothy is to read through it several times. Since the book is six chapters long, a single read-through should take twenty or thirty minutes. Note the main topics covered in the book as you scan its brief but important passages.

1. What are your first impressions of 1 Timothy? (What is it about? What seem to be its major concerns? If you had to pick a single term to describe this epistle, what would it be?)

_____

_____

_____

_____

_____

_____

_____

_____

_____

_____

2. Repetition is a clue to the ideas an author wants to stress. What key words or phrases does Paul use over and over in this epistle?

_____

_____

_____

_____

_____

Study Skill—Themes and Purposes
Before you study a book in detail, it is helpful to make some tentative conclusions about the book's themes and purposes. A *theme* is a main topic that recurs throughout the book, such as "the church." A *purpose* is a reason the author wrote the book, such as "to teach God's people how to operate in the church."
    One reading of 1 Timothy may not give you a firm sense of Paul's main themes and purposes, but by now you probably are at least beginning to have ideas about what they may be. Don't be hesitant to express those ideas; remember, they're tentative!

---

3. Look especially for the following terms. Where are they found, and how are they used throughout 1 Timothy?

a. Good _____

_____

_____

_____

b. Faith _____

_____

_____

_____

16

c. Trustworthy saying _____

_____

_____

_____

d. Teach _____

_____

_____

_____

e. Fight _____

_____

_____

_____

For Thought and Discussion: In the various epistles, Paul often talks about the Christian life as a *fight*. Why do you think he uses this image? Why not describe it in a more positive way? In what ways is it really like a fight?

4. The practice of outlining often helps tremendously in obtaining a firm grasp of the flow and general content of a book. Fill in the following "skeleton" with your own chapter and verse numbers for each section, as well as appropriate titles. A more detailed outline appears on pages 13-14.

1:1-2   Salutation

1:3-11   Warning against false teachers

_____

_____

_____

_____

1:12-20   God's grace to Paul

_____

_____

_____

_____

2:1-14   Instructions for church worship

_____

_____

_____

_____

3:1-16   Qualifications for church leadership

_____

_____

_____

_____

4:1–6:2   Instructions to Timothy

_____

_____

_____

_____

_____

_____

_____

_____

_____

6:3-10   Instructions about money

Optional Application:
What do you hope to get out of this study of 1 Timothy? What one area of your life do you think it could have the most affect on?

_____

_____

_____

_____

6:11-16   Paul's charge to Timothy

_____

_____

_____

_____

6:17-19   Instructions about the wealthy

_____

_____

_____

_____

6:20-21   Benediction

5. Note here any teachings, commands, warnings, or instructions from 1 Timothy that you want to think about this week.

_____

_____

_____

_____

_____

_____

_____

For Thought and Discussion: In many ways, it seems to make better sense to begin a letter with the writer's name rather than to end it that way. Do you agree? Why do you think we abandoned this ancient practice? Should we start it up again?

Optional Application: Make a change in your prayer life this week by addressing the Lord with a title you don't normally use. Meditate on one of the titles Paul uses in 1 Timothy—or another title used elsewhere in the Bible—and consciously use this title as you pray this week. Does it give you a better perspective on the Lord? If so, how?

6. After gaining some background on 1 Timothy on pages 11-13 and after reading this epistle several times, what questions do you have about the letter or its contents? (Does anything puzzle you? Surprise you? Alarm you?) Write your questions here and refer to them as you continue this study.

_____

_____

_____

_____

_____

_____

_____

Salutation (1 Timothy 1:1-2)

Like each of his thirteen epistles in the New Testament—and in keeping with the custom of the day, which was the opposite of our own—Paul begins 1 Timothy by writing his name (in Greek, *Paulos*).

7. How does Paul refer to himself in 1:1? Why do you think he does this, if in fact he is writing to a good friend? What does this imply about a larger audience for the letter?

_____

_____

_____

_____

8. How does Paul characterize Christ in 1:1? How does he describe God? How are these descriptions significant?

_____

_____

20

For Further Study: You can learn more about Timothy by reading 2 Timothy; Acts 16:1-5; 17:14-15; 18:5; 19:22; 20:4-5; 1 Corinthians 4:17; 16:10-11; 2 Corinthians 1:19; Philippians 2:19-24; 1 Thessalonians 3:2-3,6; and possibly Hebrews 13:23.

9. To whom does Paul address this letter in 1:2? How does Paul describe this person? How is this significant?

_____

_____

_____

_____

_____

_____

10. a. What kind of greeting does Paul give the recipient in 1:2? What is signficant about each of the items he mentions?

_____

_____

_____

_____

_____

_____

Study Skill — Summarizing the Passage
You can see whether you have understood a passage of Scripture by summarizing it in your own words. It can be helpful to write not only what the passage teaches, but also how the text relates to the main themes and purposes of the book.

21

For Thought and
Discussion: If you had
just received this letter,
what would you tell a
friend about it: "Oh, I
just received a letter
from Paul about . . ."?

b. How does this greeting compare with those in
  Paul's other letters?

_____

_____

_____

_____

_____

11. Based on what you know of 1 Timothy already,
  what would you say is the *purpose* of this letter?

_____

_____

_____

_____

12. What issues in your own life have been raised by your
  initial readings of 1 Timothy? How are you planning
  to address those issues in the coming week?

_____

_____

_____

_____

_____

13. What questions do you have about 1 Timothy that
  you would like to explore further in your study of
  the book?

_____

_____

_____

_____

_____

_____

_____

For the group

It's helpful to begin each session with a question that helps group members get to know each other better and connect their own experience to the passage they are going to discuss. You might begin this session by asking, "Tell us about a time when you were assigned a task that felt challenging and maybe somewhat daunting. It might be a task at work, at school when you were a child, a parenting task—anything that comes to mind. How did you feel when you set out to face that task? What helped you?"

As the group leader, you should answer the question first. You will set an example of how long and how personal answers should be. Limit your answer to a minute or less so as not to overwhelm your study time, and share something that was genuinely daunting for you but probably not the worst crisis of your life. Your goal is to invite the group to identify with Timothy's situation.

In this and later lessons, don't feel obliged to discuss every one of the numbered questions. You might choose just half a dozen that seem to promise the most lively and helpful discussion. Your goal in this session is to help the group see this letter as a whole.

LESSON TWO

1 TIMOTHY 1:3-11

Beware of False Teachers

As you thought about the purpose of 1 Timothy in the previous lesson, you may have noted that 1 Timothy 3:15 provides an overview of the entire book: "You will know how people ought to conduct themselves in God's household." The whole letter is about precisely that: how God's people ought to act in God's church.

Unfortunately, God's people do not always act as they should. That sad fact is trumpeted loud and clear from the very beginning of 1 Timothy. The church at Ephesus had some major problems, and that is why Paul requested that his trusted associate, Timothy, remain at the church to help it straighten out the problems and give them the tools they needed to grow in the faith.

Read through 1 Timothy 1:3-11 and note the unique challenges that faced Timothy in the church at Ephesus, as well as the strategies that Paul suggests Timothy use to overcome them.

Stay there in Ephesus (1:3). After Paul was released from his first Roman imprisonment, he apparently once more visited the church at Ephesus, where he found conditions that needed extended attention. Timothy was the right man for the job.

Myths and endless genealogies (1:4). We don't know exactly what the false teachers in Ephesus were teaching. If they were Jews, they may have devised a complex mythology based on Old Testament

25

False prophets and false teachers have always been around to plague God's people. Note just a few other references where they are named: Jeremiah 23:9-40; Ezekiel 13; Matthew 7:15-23, 24:24; Acts 13:6-12, 20:29-31; 2 Corinthians 11:13-15; Galatians 2:4; 2 Peter 2:1-3; 1 John 4:1-3.

genealogies. On the other hand, they may have been forerunners of the groups that became popular in the second century A.D. We call those groups *Gnostics* from the Greek word *gnosis,* "knowledge." Each Gnostic group claimed that one could be saved from futility only by knowing some secret knowledge which that group alone possessed. This secret knowledge they claimed centered around a complex geneology, beginning with the true "Absolute," who fathered a secondary deity, who fathered a tertiary deity or deities, and so on.

A good conscience and a sincere faith (1:5). Note the reappearance of these paired items in 1:19, 3:9.

The law (1:7-8). This refers to the Torah, the first five books of the Bible, written by Moses, also called the Pentateuch.

Those who kill their fathers or mothers (1:9). This phrase includes two words in Greek, *patroloais* and *matroloais,* which are found only here in the New Testament. Literally, the pairing of the words "father" and "mother" with the verb "to strike." Perhaps the sin here is not so much murder as it is the ultimate dishonoring of parents.

1. What was the purpose of Paul's instruction to Timothy to stay in Ephesus? What was the problem there?

_____

_____

_____

_____

2. a. To what were certain men devoted in Ephesus, according to 1 Timothy 1:4?

_____

_____

_____

_____

b. Why was this a problem? What happens when our devotion is redirected away from Christ?

_____

_____

_____

_____

_____

For Further Study: Note how often 1 Timothy deals with false doctrines or peripheral issues that lead believers away from maturity. Compare the following verses in 1 Timothy: 1:3-4; 4:1-3,7; 6:3-5, 20-21.

Study Skill — Outlining the Purpose
An ordinary outline of 1 Timothy such as the one on pages 13-14 can help you find particular passages, but it tells you little of how the parts fit into Paul's overall message. One way to recall the epistle's message at a glance is to outline the way each passage unfolds.

For instance, Paul's purpose is to give Timothy guidelines for the proper functioning of the church so that it can grow and be effective in its difficult setting. A broad outline of the book that takes account of this purpose might begin like this:

1:1-2   Salutation: Paul greets his son in the faith.

1:3-11   False Teachers of the Law: Paul warns Timothy about the dangers of false teachers of the law.

1:12-20 God's Grace to Paul: The apostle reminds Timothy that God's grace is greater than any problem he might face in Ephesus; after all, it transformed no less a violent man than Paul himself.

On separate paper begin your own outline of 1 Timothy that reflects Paul's purpose and themes. You can make up your own summaries for 1:1-20, or copy these and begin your own outline with 2:1. Add a new entry as you complete each lesson.

Be honest with yourself and ask the question, "Am I overly committed to a teaching or belief that does not lead either myself or others to greater godliness?" Be ruthless in your evaluation. Certain "pet" doctrines or beliefs may, in the final analysis, alienate fellow believers rather than helping them mature in Christ.

Optional Application:
Rather than determining right from wrong, the conscience flashes a warning to us when we *know* we are doing or are about to do wrong. In other words, we train our conscience by what we believe and are committed to.

What are you training yourself to believe? What are you committed to? How would you characterize your own conscience? Is it tender? Sensitive? Hard? Seared? Would others agree with your evaluation?

3. According to 1:4-5, what is one way to determine if a teaching is valid and true? Conversely, what is one way to determine if a teaching is false and harmful?

_____

_____

_____

_____

4. How would you define ...

a "pure heart"? _____

_____

_____

_____

a "good conscience"? _____

_____

_____

_____

a "sincere faith"? _____

_____

_____

_____

5. Do you think you possess these things? Explain.

_____

_____

_____

_____

_____

_____

6. How does someone "wander away" from the things mentioned in question 4? Do you know of anyone who has done so? Explain.

_____

_____

_____

_____

_____

_____

7. What do you suppose Paul means by the phrase "meaningless talk"? How can you tell if an idea or teaching is "meaningless"?

_____

_____

_____

_____

_____

8. a. Who is Paul describing in 1:7? What does he tell us about them?

_____

_____

_____

_____

b. Have you ever come in contact with someone who might fit into such a category? If so, describe them. How did you respond to them?

_____

_____

Optional Application: No one plans to wander or drift away from the truth; but it happens. What can you do to ensure that you won't wander away from truth? Do you have a plan to make sure you don't find yourself miles away from where you want to be spiritually? If so, what is it?

For Further Study: King Solomon talked a lot about meaninglessness. How does his use of "meaningless" in the Old Testament book of Ecclesiastes compare with what Paul has in mind in 1 Timothy? Is it different in any way? If so, how?

For Further Study:
Read Romans 1:21-22
and Titus 1:10-11. What
do these passages add
to what you learn from
1 Timothy 1:7?

Optional Application:
All of us tend to struggle
with pride in one of its
many ugly forms. Are
you ever tempted to give
an answer to a question
about the Bible, even
when you're pretty sure
you don't know what the
answer is? If so, why?

9. Why would someone want to teach something they didn't understand? Why would they "confidently affirm" something they had no real comprehension of? What problem or sin is at the root of such a dilemma?

10. a. How does Paul know that the law is "good" (1:8)?

Study Skill—Five Questions

The following five questions can help you apply God's Word to your life. When you study a passage, ask yourself:

- Is there a *sin* for me to avoid?
- Is there a *promise* for me to trust?
- Is there an *example* for me to follow?
- Is there a *command* for me to obey?
- How can this passage increase my *knowledge* of God?

You can recall these five questions by remembering the acronym SPECK—Sin, Promise, Example, Command, Knowledge.

_____

_____

b. How does one use it "properly"? How can it be used "improperly"?

_____

_____

_____

_____

_____

11. For whom is the law intended, according to 1:9-10? Explain in your own words.

_____

_____

_____

_____

For Thought and Discussion: Try to imagine what the world would be like without sin — no crime, no lying, no ill-will, no evil plotting, no harsh words, no disharmony of any kind. In such a place, would law be needed? Do laws ever control behavior that is not evil? What about speed limits? Fire codes? If you were running such a world, what kinds of laws, if any, would you enforce?

12. If persons such as those listed in 1:9-10 did not exist, would law be necessary? Why, or why not?

_____

_____

_____

_____

13. a. What is "sound doctrine" (1:10), according to Paul?

_____

_____

_____

_____

For Thought and Discussion: What is the connection between sound doctrine and godly living? Is it possible to have the latter without the former? For example, what connection does right belief about the Trinity have on your walk with Christ? How does what you believe about prophecy or "the end times" affect how you live on earth today?

Optional Application: It's one thing to understand the gospel; it's another to use it while witnessing to an unbeliever. When was the last time you shared the gospel with someone who did not know Christ? If you have not done this lately, start praying now that God would put you in a situation where you would be able to do so. But be prepared—this is a prayer God often answers in a hurry!

b. How can you tell if a doctrine today is sound or not? What "tests" does Paul mention in 1:3-11?

_____

_____

_____

_____

_____

_____

_____

14. What does Paul mean by "the glorious gospel of the blessed God" (1:11)? Does he define it here or elsewhere in 1 Timothy? See if you can name other places in his writings where he describes this more fully. Then describe this "glorious gospel" in your own words.

_____

_____

_____

_____

_____

_____

_____

15. a. What is your overall impression of 1:3-11? How is it significant that Paul starts out his letter in this way?

_____

_____

_____

_____

b. Do you think you would have enjoyed being in Timothy's sandals at Ephesus? Why, or why not?

_____

_____

_____

_____

_____

16. What questions do you have from this passage? Anything that puzzles you? Confuses you? Write down your questions and as the study continues, return to see if they are answered.

_____

_____

_____

_____

_____

_____

_____

For Thought and Discussion: Timothy had hoped that his mentor, Paul, would soon be by to help him in his difficult assignment at Ephesus, but then he found out Paul was delayed in coming. How would he feel? How would he respond to this letter? What hints or instructions would he especially be eager to receive? How would he share this letter with the people in his congregation?

For the group

As an opening question you might ask, "Would you describe yourself as a person who loves a good debate? Why, or why not?"

It's probably not necessary to understand exactly what the false teaching in Ephesus was. The important thing is that it distracted people from the essence of the gospel. Is your group a place where people can talk about teachings that they think distract people from the gospel today? Those things tend to be "hot potatoes" since one person may be passionately attached to a belief that another person thinks is wrong. Knowing your group, what do you think are some teachings that might be helpful to bring up in this context? Be prepared to referee a debate on some issues, and don't hesitate to cut a discussion short and move on when you decide that's necessary. Instead of debating the rightness or wrongness of a teaching, assess it by the standard Paul gives in this section: does it promote God's work by faith (and what does that mean, anyway)? Does it lead others toward love and good deeds (Hebrews 10:24)?

1 TIMOTHY 1:12-17

Grace!

Paul never got over the fact that at one time he had been determined to destroy God's church. Yet to him, the memory was not an occasion to revisit guilt, but one of great thankfulness to the merciful God who transformed him from a persecutor of Christ's body to an apostle of the church.

The apostle knew very well that his experience was not a solitary one; God lavished divine mercy and grace upon him in order to demonstrate what he longed to do for others. Perhaps one reason Paul wrote of his own experience at the beginning of this letter was to remind Timothy that the same grace and power God used to transform Paul was also available to him. No problem—no matter how difficult or agonizing—is beyond God's reach. Paul was a living example of this truth.

Once a blasphemer and a persecutor and a violent man (1:13). Paul, then called Saul, was a feared enemy of the church before his encounter with God. (See Acts 7:59–8:3; 9:1-5; 22:2-5, 26:9-11; Galatians 1:13.)

Trustworthy saying (1:15). Literally, "faithful the word." The phrase is found only in the pastorals. See 1 Timothy 3:1, 2 Timothy 2:11, Titus 3:8. It is used to describe statements that ought to be regarded as fully reliable.

The worst (1:15-16). Literally, "first" or "chief." No doubt the apostle gave himself this title because he

35

For Further Study: We
can learn a lot simply by
studying the various
titles used to describe
God and His Son, Jesus.
Look up the following
selection of titles and
decide what each one
adds to your under-
standing of and appreci-
ation for our Lord:
Psalm 2:2; Isaiah 9:6;
Luke 2:25; John 6:48;
1 Corinthians 15:45;
Ephesians 2:20;
Hebrews 3:1, 12:2;
1 Peter 5:4; Revelation
1:8.

Optional Application:
Do you consciously
depend on God's
strength to make it
through your days and
weeks? If so, how? If
not, why not? What
strategies do you use to
consciously depend on
God's strength and not
your own?

was the man at the forefront of efforts to destroy
the church—the heart of God's redemptive plan
for the world. Paul could think of no sin worse
than to attempt to destroy the very thing for
which Jesus Christ gave His life.

Unlimited patience (1:16). A divine attitude of moral
restraint that holds out under provocation. If anyone had provoked God's wrath, it was Paul; and
yet he was shown mercy instead of judgment.

1. a. Note that Paul calls Christ Jesus "our Lord" in
1:12. What does he mean by this?

_____

_____

_____

_____

b. What other titles does he use for Christ throughout this book (see 1:1, 2:5)? What significance
does each have?

_____

_____

_____

_____

_____

2. In what way did Christ give Paul "strength" (1:12)?
What connection does this have to Paul's being
considered "faithful"?

_____

_____

_____

_____

_____

For Thought and Discussion: Discuss as a group your own "pre-Christian" histories. What kind of words would you use to describe your behavior before you knew Christ? Are any of them similar to the description of the Apostle Paul? If so, how?

3. Compare Acts 8:1-3, 9:1-22, 22:3-5, 26:9-11 with 1 Timothy 1:13. Then match the descriptions in Acts of Paul's former behavior with the three terms mentioned in 1 Timothy.

a. Blasphemer _____

_____

_____

_____

b. Persecutor _____

_____

_____

_____

c. Violent man _____

_____

_____

_____

4. a. Why was Paul "shown mercy," according to 1:13?

_____

_____

_____

_____

_____

For Thought and Discussion: "Faith" and "love" are often paired elsewhere in the New Testament, as they are in 1 Timothy 1:14. Why do you suppose this is so? How are they related?

b. What does this reveal about God's character?

_____

_____

_____

_____

_____

_____

c. What implications, if any, does it have for evangelism?

_____

_____

_____

_____

_____

_____

5. Paul says three things were "poured out" on him in Christ Jesus (1:14). What are these three things, and what significance does each have?

_____

_____

_____

_____

_____

_____

_____

_____

_____

_____

6. a. What "trustworthy saying" does Paul cite in 1:15? Why does it deserve "full acceptance"?

_____

_____

_____

_____

_____

b. Do you have any personal experience with the truth of this saying? Explain.

_____

_____

_____

_____

_____

7. How could Paul say he was the "worst of sinners"? Do you think this was literally true—was his sin really worse than that of others—or could it be the way every deeply convicted sinner feels? Explain.

_____

_____

_____

_____

_____

_____

8. a. For what reason was Paul shown mercy, according to 1:16?

_____

_____

Optional Application: Sometimes it is good for us to consider the sin from which Christ delivered us. Paul calls himself "the worst of sinners," but without wallowing in guilt. He used it as a reminder of God's grace, not of the extent of his sin. Spend time this week considering your own sin, not to focus on your guilt but to remind yourself of the incredible grace God offered to save you from your sin.

For Thought and Discussion: If ignorance is no excuse for disobeying the law, then how can Paul say that he was granted mercy precisely because he acted in ignorance and unbelief? Compare this with Luke 12:47-48.

Optional Application:
How have you experienced Christ's patience? Spend some time thanking Him for that.

For Further Study:
Where would we be if God were not patient with us? Consider the following texts: Romans 2:4; 9:22; 1 Peter 3:20; 2 Peter 3:8-9,15.

b. What does this teach you about God's character?

_____

_____

_____

_____

9. How did Christ display His "unlimited patience" in Paul's life? In what way is 1:16 the gospel in brief?

_____

_____

_____

_____

_____

_____

10. What does each of the following terms found in 1:17 contribute to your understanding of God?

a. King _____

_____

_____

_____

b. Eternal _____

_____

_____

_____

c. Immortal _____

_____

_____

_____

d. Invisible _____

_____

_____

_____

e. Only God _____

_____

_____

_____

For Thought and Discussion: Think for a moment what it would be like to serve God if He were the *opposite* of the traits listed in 1 Timothy 1:17. In other words, what if He were not a king, but an overlord? What if He were not eternal, but 500 years old? What if He were mortal? What if you could see Him? What if He were only one of several similar gods?

Optional Application: Take some time during your study to give "honor" and "glory" to God. Think of creative ways to do this. What could you do to especially bestow honor upon God? What brings glory to Him? How could you continue to do this even after the study?

Study Skill—Application

It is often easiest to plan an application in several steps. Consider these steps:

1. What *truth* from the passage do I want to apply?
2. How is this truth *relevant* to me? How do I fall short in this area, or how do I want to grow?
3. What can I do, by God's grace, to *grow* in this area or apply this truth?

Remember to rely on God's guidance and power to choose and fulfill your application.

---

11. What does it mean to bestow "honor" and "glory" on God forever and ever? Since He already has these things, how can we bestow them on Him? Do we?

_____

_____

_____

_____

_____

_____

_____

12. What questions do you have from this passage? Does anything puzzle you? Alarm you? Surprise you?

_____

_____

_____

_____

_____

_____

_____

13. What idea or statement from this passage had the greatest impact on you? Why?

_____

_____

_____

_____

_____

14. Pick one truth from this passage that describes some part of God's character and meditate on it this week. Then write below any insights you gained from this exercise.

_____

_____

_____

_____

_____

_____

Amen (1:17). The word comes from a Hebrew root meaning "to be firm, steady, trustworthy." It is used in the Old Testament by a congregation or an individual to accept both the validity of an oath and its consequences (see Numbers 5:22, Deuteronomy 27:15-16, Jeremiah 11:5), as well as a response to a benediction. By the time of the New Testament, the word was regularly used at the close of prayers and doxologies to agree with the ideas and sentiments that had just been expressed.

For Thought and Discussion: In what sense does Paul use the term "amen" in 1 Timothy 1:17? Why is it appropriate here? Note that he also uses it in 6:16. How is he using it there? Why?

For the group

Since this section is largely about Paul's gratitude toward God, invite group members to begin the session by telling one thing for which they are grateful today. You should go first.

Let your goal in this session be to help participants appreciate the degree to which they are forgiven. It's easy to lose sight of how much we have to be grateful for. This might be a chance for you to tell each other some of your experiences of God's mercy and patience.

1 TIMOTHY 1:18-2:15

How the Church Works

After briefly alerting Timothy to the nature of the letter he is receiving and reminding him of the history of its author, Paul quickly moves on to offer a number of instructions and advisories about how best to direct the affairs of the church.

But before he gets to the meat of his instruction, the apostle thinks it wise to say a few words about Timothy's own spiritual background—how he had been specially chosen and prepared for the difficult task that lay ahead of him. Only with that reminder in view is Paul ready to move on to talk about the specifics of church operation.

Prophecies once made about you (1:18). These seem to have been prophetic utterances that pointed Timothy's way into the ministry. Paul hoped that by calling them to mind, Timothy would be inspired to successfully fight against the problems that had arisen in Ephesus.

Shipwrecked their faith (1:19). The willful decision to turn away from the truths of the gospel results in the destruction of "faith." This is a descriptive and colorful term used metaphorically here.

Hymenaeus and Alexander (1:20). These names appear in other New Testament passages (Acts 19:33; 2 Timothy 2:17, 4:14-15), but it is uncertain whether the same men are intended.

45

Handed over to Satan (1:20). At least two interpretations are possible. The phrase may refer to some illness or physical disability that Satan was allowed to inflict; or it may be used in a semi-technical sense, that these men had been removed from the sphere of the church and had been thrust outside into the realm of Satan, where they would be open to his attacks (see 1 Corinthians 5:5).

1. a. How does 1 Timothy 1:18-19 instruct Timothy to "fight the good fight"?

_____

_____

_____

_____

_____

b. What is this "fight"?

_____

_____

_____

c. Why does Paul call it a "fight"? Do you often think of this as a "fight" in your own life? Explain.

_____

_____

_____

_____

_____

2. a. A good "conscience" is mentioned in 1:5,19 and 3:9. What does it mean to have a good and clear conscience?

_____

_____

_____

_____

_____

b. How does one gain such a conscience?

_____

_____

_____

_____

_____

_____

c. How does one "reject" a good conscience? What is the result?

_____

_____

_____

_____

Optional Application:
What do you typically do when your conscience warns you that you're heading toward forbidden territory? Try an experiment this week. Whenever your conscience starts bothering you, write down the circumstances. Be honest about how you responded. Did you argue with it? Try to turn it off? Or did you respond by turning from the forbidden thing and moving toward what you knew was right? At the end of the week, tally up how many times it "went off."

3. a. How did Hymenaeus and Alexander "blaspheme" (1:20)?

_____

_____

_____

_____

b. What was the result?

_____

_____

_____

_____

For Thought and Discussion: Is it possible to blaspheme God without words? If so, how?

c. Do you think such a consequence could occur today? Explain.

_____

_____

_____

_____

_____

_____

Study Skill—Context

It is crucial to read individual commands in light of the whole passage, the entire book, and the rest of Scripture. The command, "She must be silent" (1 Timothy 2:12) is a good example. Elsewhere, Paul talks about women "praying" and even "prophesying" (1 Corinthians 11:5), and mentions that his relative "Junias" (a female name) was "outstanding among the apostles" (Romans 16:7). He also speaks approvingly of the godly teaching Timothy received from his mother and grandmother (2 Timothy 1:5, 3:14-15). Therefore, we must understand the command "be silent" in light of the larger purpose of 1 Timothy and in light of Paul's other instructions concerning women in the church. His primary concern here appears to be that church services should be conducted in an orderly and controlled fashion; chaos is to be avoided. He is not opposed to women making a sound in church, but rather he wants to lay down certain rules for services that will lead to order. He lays out his further thinking on the issue in 1 Corinthians 11:3-16.

The key concept to remember is that we should avoid taking a verse out of context in order to impose a restriction that the text does not intend to make. While we may not be able to completely understand what the apostle meant in an admittedly difficult passage, such as 1 Timothy 2:11-15, we can be sure of what he did *not* mean.

Blaspheme (1:20). "To speak impiously or irreverently of God or sacred things; to speak evil of; slander."[1]

4. First Timothy 2:1-2 gives instruction on prayer in at least three categories. Evaluate your own prayer life according to each element:

   a. Do you have a balance among the different kinds of prayer—*requests* for yourself, *praise* for God, *intercession* for others, and *thanksgiving*? In which of these areas would you like to grow?

   _____

   _____

   _____

   _____

   b. Consider those who benefit from our prayers: "kings and all those in authority." Do you pray for these people? Why, or why not?

   _____

   _____

   _____

   _____

   _____

   c. Consider the purpose of praying for authorities: that we may live peaceful, quiet, godly, holy lives. Why would praying for political leaders give us peaceful, quiet lives?

   _____

   _____

   _____

   _____

Optional Application:
While most people today no longer live under the reign of a king (or queen), some still do. Regardless of the form of government, we each live under a government headed up by people in authority. When was the last time you prayed for your country's leader? Your national elected or appointed representatives? Your state or local officials? Your city council member? Your school board representative? If it's been awhile, take some time right now to pray specifically for each one of these—and if you don't know who they are, now would be a great time to find out.

Optional Application:
What specifically can
you do to participate
with God in accomplish-
ing His great desire in
2:4?

**For Thought and
Discussion:** If it is
God's desire that every-
one be saved, and no
one can frustrate His will
(see Daniel 4:34-35),
then why is it that not
everyone is saved?

For Further Study: The
idea of a "mediator" is
crucial in the New Testa-
ment. Read and com-
pare Galatians 3:19-20;
Hebrews 8:6, 9:15,
12:24. What else do you
learn about this role?

d. Why is a peaceful, quiet life desirable for believers?

_____

_____

_____

_____

Wants all men to be saved (2:4). The statement
agrees with John 3:16 and 2 Corinthians 5:14-15
that Christ died for all. "Salvation has been pro-
vided for all, but only those who accept it are
saved."[2]

Mediator (2:5). The Greek term, *mesites*, means "one
who intervenes between two, either in order to
make or restore peace and friendship, or to form a
compact, or for ratifying a covenant."[3]

Ransom for all men (2:6). The word "ransom," *anti-
lytron*, occurs only here in the New Testament.
According to one scholar, it means "what is given
in exchange for another as the price of his redemp-
tion"[4] Christ paid the ransom to free us from the
slavery of sin; we are therefore rightfully His
possession.

---

5. a. What does God desire, according to 2:4?

_____

_____

_____

b. How can we "plug into" this desire, according to
2:1-2?

_____

_____

_____

_____

6. a. What three parties are mentioned in 2:5?

_____

_____

_____

b. Why is a "mediator" needed?

_____

_____

_____

_____

_____

7. a. How did Jesus "give himself" as a ransom (2:6)?

_____

_____

_____

_____

b. For whom was He given?

_____

_____

c. What difference does this make to us today?

_____

_____

_____

_____

_____

For Further Study: The idea of "ransom" is an Old Testament concept carried on by the New Testament writers. Read and compare the following verses: Psalm 49:7-9; Proverbs 21:18; Isaiah 43:3, 50:2; Jeremiah 31:11; Hosea 13:14; Matthew 20:28; Mark 10:45; Hebrews 9:15.

For Thought and Discussion: What is meant by "in its proper time" (2:6)? (See also Galatians 4:4-5.)

8. What does "testimony" mean in 2:6?

_____

_____

_____

_____

9. a. What was Paul's special task, according to 2:7?

_____

_____

_____

_____

b. In what way(s) was his ministry different from your own? In what way(s) is it similar?

_____

_____

_____

_____

_____

_____

Lift up holy hands (2:8). Lifting up hands in prayer is often mentioned in the Old Testament (see 1 Kings 8:22; Psalm 141:2, 143:6) to indicate earnest desire. The word *holy* here means "devout, pious, pleasing to God."[5]

10. a. Why is prayer incompatible with "anger" or "disputing" (2:8)?

_____

_____

_____

b. Why do you suppose this command was necessary?

_____

_____

_____

_____

_____

11. What is the main point of 2:9-10? Is Paul primarily interested in what women wear, or in something else? Explain.

_____

_____

_____

_____

_____

_____

_____

For Thought and Discussion: Is Paul saying in 1 Timothy 2:9-10 that we should wear drab clothes to worship services? That is the way the church in Russia has traditionally understood this verse, so bright clothes are seldom worn in services there. Should we "dress up" for church to show that we're giving God our best, or should we "dress down" to show our disinterest in things of this world? Which attitude are you most drawn to? Explain.

I do not permit a woman to teach (2:12). The apostle is probably giving instruction only about teaching formally in the public assemblies of the church; certainly Paul appreciated the fact that Timothy's own mother and grandmother taught him the way of God from childhood (see 2 Timothy 1:5, 3:15). Paul also expected—and accepted—that women were praying and prophesying (presumably aloud) in the worship assemblies in Corinth (1 Corinthians 11:5).

She must be silent (2:12). The identical phrase, Greek *en hesychia*, used in the previous verse was translated "in quietness"—as opposed to confusion in the public services (see 1 Corinthians 14:33).

Women will be saved through childbearing (2:15). A puzzling verse open to many interpretations, none fully satisfying. The verb "to save" is used in the New Testament both for physical healing and spiritual salvation. At least three common interpretations have been suggested: (1) the term "childbearing" refers to the birth of Christ, through whom salvation has come to the world; (2) the verse is related to Genesis 3:15, in which the seed of the woman would crush the serpent's head and bring salvation to mankind; (3) by giving birth to children, women would be saved from the social ills of the time and so take part in the mission and testimony of the church.

---

12. a. What does Paul command in 2:11-15? State what you believe he is saying in your own words.

_____

_____

_____

_____

_____

_____

b. What rationale does he give for his commands?

_____

_____

_____

_____

c. What points of controversy do his words raise?

_____

_____

_____

_____

_____

d. What statements are unclear to you?

_____

_____

_____

_____

_____

_____

_____

_____

For Thought and Discussion: Why do you think Paul goes back to the Genesis creation account to support his teaching about women's role in the church? What is he trying to get at? How could a person answer someone who replied, "Well, it's true that Eve was deceived—but Adam chose sin deliberately! How does that make him a better example as a spiritual leader than Eve?"

For the group

Depending on the make-up of your group, this has the potential to be an explosive session because of the difficult teaching in 1 Timothy 2:11-15. It will be important to discuss this paragraph in the context of the whole passage, in which the theme (contrary to the effect this passage often has) is peace and quiet. We pray for governments to provide us with the environment that will allow quiet lives, men are to pray without quarreling, and women are to learn without arguing. Some possible discussion questions: "What situations in Ephesus might have prompted such comments on quietness? Should we value peacefulness in our churches today? Does that mean peace at any price, stifling all debate?"

An opening question might be, "On a scale of 0 to 5, how peaceful would you say your life is right now? Why?"

1. *Random House College Dictionary*, revised edition (New York: Random House, Inc., 1988), "blaspheme," p. 142.
2. Ralph Earle, "1, 2 Timothy," *The Expositor's Bible Commentary, Volume 11*, gen. ed. Frank E. Gaebelein (Grand Rapids: Zondervan, 1978), p. 358.
3. Earle, p. 358.
4. Earle, p. 358.
5. Earle, p. 360.

1 TIMOTHY 3:1-13

Officers in the Church

No church can operate for long without a capable leadership team at the helm. Therefore Paul set down general guidelines for choosing people capable of doing the job.

No one, of course, is perfect; but Paul laid out some fairly lofty qualifications for those who would desire to become part of the church's leadership team. If character has tended to count for less and less in secular leadership, it continues to count for a great deal in those who would hold office in the church. It is certainly not for everybody—especially the calling to teach. As another author of Scripture reminds us, "Not many of you should presume to be teachers, my brothers, because you know that we who teach will be judged more strictly" (James 3:1).

Overseer (3:1). The *King James Version* translates the Greek term, *episkope*, "the office of a bishop." It means "office of overseer" and is used in this sense in Acts 1:20.

Above reproach (3:2). Literally, "not to be laid hold of," Greek *anepilemptos*, used here and in 5:7 and 6:14. As it stands at the head of a list of qualifications, it serves as a general description of the sort of man who could meet the requirements of the office; it is not a demand of perfection.

Husband of but one wife (3:2). Either a man who has been married only once, or more likely, a man who

57

For Thought and Discussion: When Paul writes, "Here is a trustworthy saying," does that mean his other sayings and instructions aren't as trustworthy? If you want someone to pay special attention to a statement you make, what do you say? What gets their attention?

For Thought and Discussion: Personal desire is frequently connected with holding office in the church. For example, see 1 Peter 5:2. Why do you think this is true? Why is desire to lead especially important in the church?

is monogamous—only one wife at a time, and completely faithful to her.

Good reputation with outsiders (3:7). Literally, "a good testimony from those outside." A bad reputation in the community quickly leads to a bad reputation for the church, which would demean the cause of Christ.

1. Paul used the phrase "trustworthy saying" in 1:15, 3:1, 4:9 (and in 2 Timothy 2:11 and Titus 3:8). What is the point of this phrase? How is it used each time it appears?

_____

_____

_____

_____

_____

_____

_____

2. a. How is personal desire connected with the office of overseer in 3:1? Why is it important?

_____

_____

_____

_____

_____

b. How could such a desire be easily perverted?

_____

_____

_____

_____

3. In what way is being an overseer a "noble task"?

_____

_____

_____

_____

4. What do you think Paul meant when he used the term "above reproach"?

_____

_____

_____

_____

_____

5. Paul used the following terms to establish qualifications for those who want to become overseers in the church. How does each qualification help make a better leader?

husband of but one wife _____

_____

_____

temperate _____

_____

_____

self-controlled _____

_____

_____

respectable_____

_____

_____

Optional Application: If being an overseer is a noble task, it ought to be recognized as such by those who benefit from the overseer's work—those of us in the church. Think of a way to honor those who serve the church where you attend. Let them know this week that you believe what they are doing is indeed a noble task.[1]

For Thought and Discussion: If you listed the qualifications for church leadership—without 1 Timothy 3 to guide you—what would you write? What qualities would you stress? What kind of background? What situation in life? What sort of tests might you provide? When you're finished, compare your list to Paul's. How similar are they? Where do they differ? Why?

Scripture exhorts children to respect their parents. See Exodus 20:12, Leviticus 19:3, Deuteronomy 5:16, Matthew 15:4, Ephesians 6:1-3. But Paul instructs Timothy that an elder is responsible to see that his children respect him. How can this be done?

For Thought and Discussion: Paul's comment in 1 Timothy 3:5 is often ignored today, with unfortunate results. What do you think is the vital connection between managing a family well and managing a church well? Why do you think this connection is ignored?

hospitable _____

_____

_____

able to teach _____

_____

_____

not given to drunkenness _____

_____

_____

not violent but gentle _____

_____

_____

not quarrelsome _____

_____

_____

not a lover of money _____

_____

_____

manages his own family well _____

_____

_____

not a recent convert _____

_____

_____

has a good reputation with outsiders _____

_____

_____

6. Why would it be important for an overseer to "see that his children obey him with proper respect"? What connection is there between this and directing the affairs of the church?

_____

_____

_____

_____

_____

_____

7. What do you think is Paul's logic behind his statement in 3:5?

_____

_____

_____

_____

8. a. What dangers could a young convert be exposed to if he were given a leadership role within the church?

_____

_____

_____

_____

_____

b. What modern-day applications of this principle (beyond qualifications for being an overseer) can you think of?

_____

_____

Optional Application: New converts become mature enough to serve in a leadership role by learning from more mature believers. A mature Christian must take a new convert under his wing and "show him the ropes." There are more new believers who desire such a relationship than there are mature believers willing to give of their time.

Have you ever considered discipling someone else? If not, why not? If so, what can you do right now to begin preparing for such a partnership? What steps do you need to take to begin readying a young believer for a significant place in the church?

Optional Application:
Have you ever wondered what your own reputa-tion is outside the walls of your home church? If you really want to know, either ask people directly, or ask a friend to do the asking for you (you might get more honest results this way). Find out what nonChris-tians think of your repu-tation as a citizen, neighbor, parent, etc. But be warned—if you don't like what you hear, don't take it out on them! Rather, take what-ever steps are necessary to improve your standing in the community.

9. Why is it important for an overseer to have a "good reputation with outsiders"? How would the lack of such a reputation make it easier for someone to "fall into disgrace" and "into the devil's trap"?

_____

_____

_____

_____

_____

_____

Deacons (3:8). Most simply this Greek word, *diakonos*, means "servant." Acts 6 provides the model for this office.

Much wine (3:8). Similar to the qualification for over-seer in 3:3, but a longer and stronger expression. Leaders in the church should certainly never be prone to even a hint of drunkenness.

10. First Timothy 3:8-13 lists several qualifications for becoming a deacon. Discuss each one, comparing them with the qualifications for overseers.

worthy of respect_____

_____

_____

sincere _____

_____

_____

not indulging in much wine _____

_____

_____

not pursuing dishonest gain _____

_____

_____

keeps hold of the deep truths of the faith _____

_____

_____

clear conscience _____

_____

_____

husband of but one wife _____

_____

_____

manages his children and household well _____

_____

_____

_____

For Thought and Discussion: Some people assert that the word *much* in 1 Timothy 3:8 makes it highly unlikely that the "wine" spoken of in this passage refers to grape juice, as is contended by some interpreters. Do you agree? Explain. Do you think it's acceptable for church leaders to drink alcohol? Why, or why not?

Optional Application: Design a "test" for someone who is under consideration for the office of deacon. What kind of test do you think is fair? What kind of test would you be willing to undergo?

11. Paul says that men who are under consideration for becoming deacons must first be "tested" (3:10). What kind of test do you think he has in mind? What sort of test would be appropriate?

_____

_____

_____

_____

12. First Timothy 3:11 lists several qualifications for the wives of deacons. Determine the importance of each.

    worthy of respect_____

    _____

    _____

    not malicious talkers_____

    _____

    _____

    temperate _____

    _____

    _____

    trustworthy in everything_____

    _____

    _____

13. Why do you think it would be important for both a deacon and his wife to possess certain qualities, but not others?

    _____

    _____

    _____

    _____

    _____

    _____

    _____

14. Paul says that deacons who serve well "gain an excellent standing and great assurance in their faith." Why do you suppose this is? Does this apply only to deacons, or to others as well? Explain.

_____

_____

_____

_____

_____

_____

Optional Application: Although you may not be a candidate for overseer or deacon, the qualities listed are to be desired in each of our lives. Which single quality causes you the most struggle? Explain. Which quality do you best embody? How has this occurred? Choose a quality that you would most like to work on and pray about it every day this week. Then develop a plan for working toward acquiring that trait in your life.

15. What questions do you have about 3:1-13? Write them here and discuss them as a group, or return to them after you have completed the study.

_____

_____

_____

_____

_____

_____

_____

For the group

Because this passage centers around leadership within the church, ask group members to name a great leader they admire and tell why.

This session has the potential to cause heated discussion over the roles women should take in the church. Remember that the people in your group may have strong opinions on this subject and, as the leader, help them listen to each other without interrupting. Emphasize that regardless of one's view the leadership qualities Paul gives are suitable for any leader, whether in the church or not. Your goal for this session is to understand the qualities a leader should have.

1. For more ideas about how you can support those in leadership at your church, see Wes Roberts' book, *Support Your Local Pastor* (Colorado Springs, Colo.: NavPress, 1995).

1 TIMOTHY 3:14–4:16

A Word to Timothy

Paul hoped to be with Timothy soon after he wrote this letter, but he knew his plans often changed unexpectedly—whether by his own doing, by circumstances, or by God. So as a precaution Paul penned several instructions to Timothy that would help him get the church at Ephesus on the right track.

Before he got to the specifics, Paul thought it wise to remind Timothy of the glorious Lord they both served. He knew how easy it is to get discouraged when we take our eyes off the source of our strength and success! Yet he also knew how effective we can be when we remind ourselves of the glory of our great God and Savior.

From this point on in his letter, Paul ranges freely from problem to instruction to encouragement and back again. He seldom goes into great lengths in any of his instruction, for no doubt Timothy had already received ample instruction. Nevertheless, because of the difficult ministry in Ephesus, Paul considered it best to sketch for Timothy an outline of what it would take to get Ephesus "up and running" in a way that would honor and glorify God.

Mystery of godliness (3:16). The phrase means the "revealed secret of true piety," or the secret that produces real piety in believers. The context reveals that this secret is Jesus Christ.

67

For Further Study:
Several names are used
in Scripture to describe
the church, among
them: the body of Christ
(1 Corinthians 12:12-27);
the bride of Christ (Rev-
elation 19:7); a spiritual
house (1 Peter 2:5); the
Israel of God (Galatians
6:16). What do you
learn about the church
from each of these
images?

For Further Study: The
word *mystery* is a
favorite term of Paul's.
What kind of "mysteries"
does he speak of in
each of the following
passages: Romans
11:25; 16:25; 1 Corin-
thians 13:2; 14:2;
15:51; Ephesians 1:9;
3:3-4,6,9; 5:32.

He appeared in a body (3:16). Some ancient manuscripts read, "*God* appeared in a body" (see the
   King James Version), but the oldest manuscripts
   all use the term *hos* ("who" or "he"), not *theos*
   ("God"). The phrase is a reference to the incarna-
   tion of Christ.

1. Paul gives several names to the church in 1 Timothy 3:15. What does each term add to your understanding of the body of Christ?

   a. God's household _____

   _____

   _____

   _____

   b. The church of the living God _____

   _____

   _____

   _____

   c. The pillar and foundation of the truth _____

   _____

   _____

   _____

2. Why is "the mystery of godliness" that Paul writes
   about in 3:16 "great" beyond all question?

   _____

   _____

   _____

   _____

   _____

   _____

3. First Timothy 3:16 is apparently an ancient hymn composed about Christ. What does each stanza of the hymn teach you about Christ? See if you can locate other Scripture references that support your assertions.

a. He appeared in a body _____

_____

_____

_____

b. He was vindicated by the Spirit _____

_____

_____

_____

c. He was seen by angels _____

_____

_____

_____

d. He was preached among the nations _____

_____

_____

_____

e. He was believed on in the world _____

_____

_____

_____

f. He was taken up in glory _____

_____

_____

_____

Optional Application:
The hymn in 1 Timothy 3:16 provides a perfect outline for a week's meditation on who Christ is and what He has done for us. Meditate on a different stanza each day of the week—turning over in your mind the meaning and significance of what Christ did for you—then on the seventh day meditate on the whole passage and give thanks to Jesus that He loved you enough to do all this for you.

For Further Study:
Read 2 Timothy 3:1-9
and compare it with
1 Timothy 4:1. Does it
appear that these texts
describe the same time
period? Why, or why
not? How can you tell?

**For Thought and
Discussion:** A hypocrite
is someone who pro-
fesses one thing but
lives another, a "person
who pretends to have
desirable or publicly
approved attitudes,
beliefs, principles, etc.,
he does not actually
possess."[1] Often we
can't tell when *we're*
being hypocritical. Why
do you think this is?
Why is it harder to admit
we're being hypocrites
than it is to admit having
a temper or to lying?
Why does the Bible so
strongly condemn
hypocrisy? (See
Matthew 23:23,25,
27,29; Luke 12:1; Titus
1:16.)

In later times (4:1). The expression is not as strong as
the phrase used in 2 Timothy 3:1, "in the last
days." Evidently the conditions described here
took place during Paul's lifetime.

*Forbid people to marry and order them to abstain
from certain foods* (4:3). Such an ascetic emphasis made its way into the church in the first century and became quite popular in the second
century. The error was the equation of holiness
with self-denial.

Godless myths and old wives' tales (4:7). Literally,
"profane and old-womanish myths." Paul equates
these teachings with the fairy tales that elderly
women love to tell children; they have no basis in
reality.

4. a. Where did Paul get his knowledge of "later
times"? How certain is this knowledge?

_____

_____

_____

   b. What difference does it make? Why is it important that we should know it?

_____

_____

_____

5. How does Paul characterize the false teachers of
4:2? Do they know that what they are teaching is
false? Explain.

_____

_____

_____

_____

_____

6. a. What orders did these teachers give their followers (4:3)?

_____

_____

_____

_____

b. What was wrong with these orders?

_____

_____

_____

_____

7. What is the main point of 4:4-5?

_____

_____

_____

_____

8. a. How was Timothy to respond to these false teachings (4:6)?

_____

_____

_____

_____

b. What example does this suggest for us?

_____

_____

_____

_____

For Thought and Discussion: In these health-conscious days, some people are dismayed by Paul's words in 1 Timothy 4:4-5 because they believe he's teaching that all foods are created equal. But is this true? Does this verse teach that all foods are equally healthy to eat, or is its point something else? Consider especially the word *consecrated* in 4:5.

Optional Application: When you are faced with what you know (not just suspect) is false teaching, how do you react? What do you do? Do you let it go, or are you more likely to confront the problem head-on? How do you think you should respond? How can you train yourself to respond more along those lines?

For Thought and Discussion: When you hear the word *godly*, what picture comes to mind? Why? Who is the most godly person you know personally? What makes this person godly? How can you pursue godliness? See Psalm 4:3, 32:6; Acts 8:2; 2 Corinthians 7:10-11, 11:2; 2 Timothy 3:12; Titus 2:12; 2 Peter 2:9, 3:11.

Optional Application: What kind of physical training do you do? What kind of godliness training do you do? Which of the two do you spend the most time on? If you were to plan out a physical training schedule for yourself, what would it look like? A godliness training schedule? What steps can you take to implement these schedules?

9. a. What is Timothy to avoid in 4:7? Why? What is he to pursue instead?

_____

_____

_____

_____

_____

b. How could he, and we, do this practically?

_____

_____

_____

_____

_____

10. What comparison does Paul make between "physical training" and "godliness training" in 4:8? How easy is it for you to keep the proper balance? Explain.

_____

_____

_____

_____

_____

Savior of all men, and especially of those who believe (4:10). This is a debated statement, but one that cannot promise universal salvation. Even in this letter Paul maintains that faith is necessary for salvation. The phrase probably means that through Calvary, God is *potentially* the Savior of all men, but only those who believe will be *finally* saved.

Elders laid their hands on you (4:14). Apparently a service where the body of elders (*presbyterion*) placed their hands on Timothy and prophesied over him. Similar references are found in 1:18 and 2 Timothy 1:6.

Save both yourself and your hearers (4:16). "For a soul-winner to save others and lose his own soul is an unmitigated tragedy. For one to save his own soul and have his hearers lost is no less tragic. We must give attention to both."[2]

---

11. For what did Paul "labor and strive" in 4:10? In what sense did he labor and strive for this—to gain it, or for some other reason?

_____

_____

_____

_____

12. How is God "the Savior of all men"? What is special about "those who believe"? How would you answer those who contend that this verse teaches the universal salvation of all humanity?

_____

_____

_____

_____

_____

_____

13. a. Why might others look down on Timothy (4:12)?

_____

_____

Optional Application: Is there anything in your life for which you can honestly say that you "labor and strive"? What do you think you *should* be laboring and striving for? What would it take for you to change your habits or behavior, if that is required?

For Thought and Discussion: "Universalists" believe that everyone will ultimately be saved. They take passages such as Luke 23:34, Romans 5:18, 1 Timothy 4:10, and 2 Peter 3:9 and teach that no one ultimately will be lost. How would you answer such a contention?

Optional Application:
Grade yourself on the five aspects of a believer's conduct that Paul mentions in 1 Timothy 5:12. On a scale from 1 (poor) to 5 (excellent), what grade would you give yourself in: (a) speech; (b) life; (c) love; (d) faith; (e) purity? What do your grades suggest you need to do, if anything?

_____

_____

b. How was he to counteract this tendency?

_____

_____

_____

_____

14. Paul notes five aspects of a believer's conduct that are especially important in setting a good example for others. What does he mean by each, and what is important about each of them?

a. Speech _____

_____

_____

_____

b. Life_____

_____

_____

_____

c. Love _____

_____

_____

_____

d. Faith _____

_____

_____

_____

e. Purity _____

_____

_____

_____

Optional Application: What kind of progress are people around you seeing you make? Is it obvious so that people can't help but see? Explain.

15. To what was Timothy to devote himself in Paul's absence (4:13-14)? What is so critical about each of these activities?

_____

_____

_____

_____

_____

_____

16. What reason does Paul give in 4:15 for diligence in pursuing the ministry? What did Paul want to see happen? Why was this important?

_____

_____

_____

_____

_____

_____

17. a. What charge did Paul give Timothy in 4:16?

_____

_____

_____

_____

75

b. What reason did he give for the charge? How is this the same for us today?

_____

_____

_____

_____

_____

18. Write down any questions you have about this passage. Discuss them as a group, and return to them later if any continue to puzzle you.

_____

_____

_____

_____

_____

_____

_____

For the group

In this section, Paul instructs Timothy on a variety of subjects. One thing he warns Timothy about is false teaching. Begin your session by asking group members to describe a false teaching they have been exposed to and how they responded.

Let your goal for this session be to help group members learn practical ways they can "conduct themselves in God's household, which is the church of the living God" (1 Timothy 3:15).

1. *Random House College Dictionary*, revised edition (New York: Random House, Inc., 1988), "hypocrite," p. 653.
2. Ralph Earle, "1, 2 Timothy," *The Expositor's Bible Commentary, Volume 11*, gen. ed. Frank E. Gaebelein (Grand Rapids: Zondervan, 1978), p. 375.

1 TIMOTHY
5:1–6:2

Various Instructions

Numerous activities occur in any church, regardless of where it is, how large the congregation is, or how old the church is. Such activity inevitably brings up important questions: How should a young pastor treat older members? How should he treat members close to his own age? What should be done about the needs of widows? How do you tell if someone is truly in need of the church's assistance? How should faithful elders be rewarded for their service? What do you do about elders who sin? And what can be done for an upset stomach?

While some of these issues may not seem terribly spiritual, all of them (and others like them, just as pressing) must be dealt with in a growing church. Paul knew this, and so he prepared a list of instructions and guidelines for his young associate. Of course, he hoped to be with Timothy in person before too long—but if that trip was delayed, he intended to give the young man the benefit of his long ministry experience. His words no doubt were invaluable to Timothy, as they continue to be for us today.

Dead even while she lives (5:6). Physically alive but
   spiritually dead. The implication is that such a
   woman has no claim on the church's support.

Denied the faith and is worse than an unbeliever
   (5:8). There is more than one way to deny the
   faith. A heretic does it by words; the person here

77

Optional Application:
Which group is it easiest
for you to interact
with—older men, older
women, younger men, or
younger women? Why
do you think this is so?
Do you put into practice
the guidelines Paul lays
down in 5:1-2? Explain.

does it by his life (see Titus 1:16). Even unbelievers
take care of their own, and they do not have the
example of Jesus Christ.

Broken their first pledge (5:12). Literally, "disre-
garded or set aside their solemn promise or oath."
Apparently such women had promised to be
devoted only to Christ, but abandoned that
promise by remarrying.

Turned away to follow Satan (5:15). The phrase does
not have to mean formal apostasy from Christianity, but does at least suggest a carnal lifestyle.

1. Paul instructs us how to treat those around us
   (5:1-2). How do these instructions differ from one
   another, and why do you think they differ? What is
   appropriate about each of them?

   a. Older men _____

   _____

   _____

   _____

   b. Younger men _____

   _____

   _____

   _____

   c. Older women _____

   _____

   _____

   _____

   d. Younger women _____

   _____

   _____

   _____

78

2. Paul's instructions about how to handle the needs of widows take up more verses than any other topic in this epistle (fourteen verses, 5:3-16). Why do you suppose this issue was so important to him?

_____

_____

_____

_____

_____

_____

3. Why would Paul say that a widow with children or grandchildren was not "really in need" (5:3-4)? Does our culture live by such reasoning? Explain.

_____

_____

_____

_____

_____

4. a. How can we practically put our "religion into practice" (5:4,16)? What does God think about this?

_____

_____

_____

_____

_____

_____

Optional Application: Does your fellowship of believers have an official policy toward widows and their care, or are cases considered on an individual basis? Talk to those who oversee such a ministry to find out how you can help.

For Thought and Discussion: Even today, widows have unique needs that "slip through the cracks." What needs have you seen go unmet? How could your church or service organization help?

For Further Study: Using a Bible dictionary, find out about the hardships for widows in Bible times. What is different from what we might expect today? What is similar? Then look at these passages to get a glimpse of the Bible's concern for widows: Exodus 22:22-24; Deuteronomy 10:18, 24:19-21; Isaiah 1:17; Zechariah 7:10; Mark 12:42-43; Acts 6:1; James 1:27.

For Thought and Discussion: We often use phrases like "hope in God" (5:5), but what does it really mean? How do you hope in God? Is any action required, or is it simply a mental exercise? How can you tell if someone is hoping in God? What can you do to put your hope in God?

Optional Application: Paul alludes in 1 Timothy 5:12 to a pledge of dedication that widows sometimes made to the Lord. Note that there is nothing wrong with such a pledge—the only problem is in breaking it.

Have you ever made a pledge to the Lord? Did you keep it? Is there some kind of pledge that you would like to make to the Lord? If so, what is it? What reason would you have for making it? And what steps could you take to make sure that you kept it?

b. How is 5:8 the other side of the coin to this instruction?

_____

_____

_____

_____

5. What contrasts are made between 5:5 and 5:6? How are they significant?

_____

_____

_____

_____

_____

6. List the seven qualifications Paul gives for a widow to be put on a church's list of widows (5:9-10). What is important about each one?

_____

_____

_____

_____

_____

_____

_____

_____

_____

_____

7. a. What reasons does Paul give for not putting younger widows on such a list (5:11-13)?

_____

_____

_____

_____

_____

b. What advice does he give instead (5:14)? What does he mean by saying that some had "turned away to follow Satan"? Can you support your answer with other Scripture references?

_____

_____

_____

_____

_____

_____

_____

Optional Application: What does your church do to "doubly honor" those whose preach and teach? What have you done, personally, to honor these people? It needn't be an elaborate thing; perhaps it's inviting someone over to dinner, taking them out to a special function, or sending them a card telling them of your appreciation for their work.

For Further Study: Note the following texts where the requirement of having two or three witnesses is stressed: Deuteronomy 17:6-7, 19:15; Matthew 18:16; 2 Corinthians 13:1; Hebrews 10:28.

Double honor (5:17). Some believe this suggests a "double stipend" or "double salary," but it may also mean double honor in the sense of recognition (rather than a financial honorarium).

Two or three witnesses (5:19). The last part of this verse comes close to a word-for-word quote of Deuteronomy 19:15. See also 2 Corinthians 13:1.

The elect angels (5:21). Paul is fond of such terms and uses them to heighten the sense of importance of the declaration he is making. See also 1 Corinthians 4:9 and 1 Timothy 3:16.

Use a little wine (5:23). Safe drinking water was not always easily obtainable; Paul's advice also may be medicinal in nature.

For Further Study: In Galatians 2:11-14 we find Paul putting into practice the directive he gives Timothy in 1 Timothy 5:20. Why did Paul do this? What transpired? What was the result? In what way is this a model for us to follow? In what ways (if any) might it not be such a model?

For Further Study: Favoritism is often denounced in the Scriptures. See Exodus 23:3, Leviticus 19:15, Romans 2:11, Ephesians 6:9, James 2:1-13.

8. a. What principle does Paul introduce in 5:17? How does he support this principle in 5:18?

_____

_____

_____

_____

_____

b. Why do you think preaching and teaching are singled out for special attention?

_____

_____

_____

9. What is the proper way to bring an accusation against an elder, according to 5:19? Why this stipulation?

_____

_____

_____

_____

_____

_____

_____

10. a. Why are elders who sin supposed to be rebuked *publicly* (5:20)? Why should they be treated differently from others?

_____

_____

_____

_____

b. In what ways does our culture often reverse this directive? Why do you think we do so?

_____

_____

_____

_____

_____

11. What charge is given to Timothy in 5:21? How is this charge made to be solemn? How is Timothy to carry out the charge?

_____

_____

_____

_____

_____

_____

12. What is the connection between "the laying on of hands" and "do not share in the sins of others" in 5:22? What principle is Paul developing here?

_____

_____

_____

_____

For Thought and Discussion: Why do you think the laying on of hands is such an important symbolic action in the Bible? What does it demonstrate? Read the following texts to get a better understanding of what this practice entails: Numbers 27:23; Luke 4:40; Acts 6:6, 8:18; 2 Timothy 1:6; Hebrews 6:1-2.

For Thought and Discussion: Paul describes a puzzling circumstance in 1 Timothy 5:24, but doesn't explain it. This verse tells us that some men are judged for their sins long before they stand in judgment before the throne of God; but it also says that other men commit grievous sins and yet are never caught and judged in this life. Why do you think God allows this? Consider what David had to say in Psalm 73.

13. What contrast is made in 5:24? Why would this be important for a church official to remember?

_____

_____

_____

_____

For Thought and Discussion: Why do you think a believing "slave" would be more likely to disrespect a "master" who was a fellow believer than if the master were not a believer at all? What principle is at work here? Have you seen it at work in your own life or home? If so, explain. See Matthew 13:57 and John 4:44.

14. What is the main point of 5:25? How have you seen this evidenced?

_____

_____

_____

_____

_____

15. a. What general principle does Paul lay out for slaves in 6:1-2? What is the primary reason he gives for enforcing this principle?

_____

_____

_____

_____

_____

_____

b. How would this instruction be important for church unity in ancient Ephesus? How would it be applicable today?

_____

_____

_____

_____

_____

16. If you have any unanswered questions from this passage of Scripture, write them down here. Discuss them as a group and if some remain unanswered, return to them later in the study after you have had a chance to do some research on your own.

_____

_____

_____

_____

_____

_____

_____

_____

For the group

In this passage, Paul continues to instruct Timothy on everything from how to treat older people to what to do for an upset stomach. His main focus, though, is on the care of widows.

Begin this session by asking, "What do you believe about caring for aging family members? Have you cared for an aging parent or relative? What was your experience?"

1 TIMOTHY 6:3-10,17-19

The Love of Money

Money—it was one of Jesus' most frequent topics, it often comes up in the Proverbs, and it was at the heart of an incident that shaped and shook up the early church (see Acts 5). Money has the power to be used for great good or to corrupt monstrously.

As Paul wrapped up his letter to Timothy, he felt the need to instruct his young associate about the proper and improper use of money in the church. He had seen with his own eyes how money can cause the downfall of believers, and he did not want that to happen in the church at Ephesus. So Paul used rather strong terms to remind Timothy about the seriousness of people's attitudes toward money.

Perhaps unsurprisingly, his words sound remarkably appropriate today. Note especially in this passage how Paul alternately warns against the improper use and view of money, and how he instructs Timothy in its effective and godly use.

A root of all kinds of evil (6:10). Literally, "a root of all the evils." Note that it is not money itself that is such a root, but the love of money. The verse is often misquoted.

---

1. How does Paul depict someone who teaches false doctrines and who does not agree to sound instruction (6:4)? List the three characteristics he names and discuss the significance of each.

For Further Study: In Scripture false teachers are often connected with illicit financial dealings. Compare 1 Timothy 6:5 with Luke 20:47, Acts 20:30-35, and 2 Peter 2:1-3. What do you learn from comparing these texts?

_____

_____

_____

_____

_____

_____

_____

2. What is the result of the kind of behavior discussed in question 1? List each of the five results that Paul names and discuss the significance of each (6:4-5).

_____

_____

_____

_____

_____

_____

_____

_____

_____

3. Note the irony Paul points out that the very men who are consumed with financial gain have been "robbed" of the truth (6:5). If it is always better to be rich in truth rather than material possessions, why are so many people tempted to put finances above truth?

_____

_____

_____

_____

4. a. How do disputes about money create "constant friction"? What is the source of this friction?

_____

_____

_____

_____

   b. What might this say about couples who often fight about finances? How can they bring back harmony?

_____

_____

_____

_____

_____

5. a. If godliness is not a means to financial gain, what kind of gain does godliness bring (6:6)? What does this verse mean to you?

_____

_____

_____

_____

   b. Is it easy for you to live this out? Explain.

_____

_____

_____

_____

6. In 1 Timothy 6:7 Paul gives a reason for his statement in 6:6. What is this reason? How would remembering his words in verse 7 help to keep us from being robbed of the truth (6:5)?

Optional Application: Which do you think you value more: truth or financial gain? Would your family agree with you? Would your friends? Explain.

For Thought and Discussion: Why do you think that television evangelists have such a bad reputation when it comes to money? Try an experiment. Watch such an evangelist and see whether he or she communicates the message that "godliness is a means to financial gain." What do you find?

For Further Study: The Scripture is full of verses about the value and necessity of contentment. Look up the following passages: Ecclesiastes 4:8, Luke 3:14, Philippians 4:11-12, Hebrews 13:5-6.

For Thought and Discussion: You may have heard it said that "there are no U-Hauls behind hearses." How is this basically the same message as 1 Timothy 6:7? How should that affect how we live?

For Thought and Discussion: While 1 Timothy 6:8 does not require believers to get rid of everything but food and clothing, it does stress an ethic that is far removed from contemporary ideas about comfort and affluence. Do you know of anyone who lives by this ethic? Does it seem other-worldly to you? How can you make it more a part of your own lifestyle today?

For Further Study: The Bible talks a great deal about not setting our hearts on money. Consider the following texts: Psalm 39:6-7, 49:10-15; Proverbs 11:28, 23:5, 28:20; Matthew 13:22; Mark 10:17-31; James 5:1-6; Revelation 3:17-18.

7. How many people you know are content with the provisions listed in 6:8? Would you be content with these things alone? Explain.

8. What warning does Paul give in 6:9-10? To whom is the warning given? What is often the result of ignoring this warning?

9. Notice the *New International Version* translates 6:10 as "the love of money is *a* root of *all kinds of* evil," rather than the traditional, "the love of money is *the* root of *all* evil" (emphasis added). What is the main point of such a translation? What do you think the translators were trying to stress, and what were they trying to avoid?

10. According to 6:10, what two things often happen to people who eagerly seek after wealth? Of the two, which do you think is worse? Which do you think people fear most? Explain.

_____

_____

_____

_____

_____

Hope in God (6:17). While wealth is uncertain and may be gone in a moment, God is immutable and immovable and has promised to be with the believer always (see Psalm 52:7, Hebrews 13:5-6).

11. Paul gives two negative commands and five positive commands to the rich in 6:17-18. List and discuss each one.

a. Negative commands _____

_____

_____

_____

_____

b. Positive commands _____

_____

_____

_____

_____

For Thought and Discussion: When Paul says that the love of money "is a root of all kinds of evil," what do you think he has in mind? What "kinds of evil" have you seen the love of money spawn?

Optional Application: What steps can you take *right now* to ensure that a desire for money will not cause you to wander away from the faith? What kind of steps *are* you taking?

For Thought and Discussion: Why do you think it is so easy for most of us to put our hope in wealth? And why is it so hard for us to put our hope in God?

For Further Study: A common biblical motivation for being "generous and willing to share" is that, in this way, we will be providing for ourselves later in God's Kingdom. Consider the following verses: Matthew 6:1-4,19-21; Luke 12:33; 2 Corinthians 9:6-11; Colossians 3:23-24.

12. According to 6:17, why is putting your hope in God the only way to "richly" enjoy life? What does the last part of this verse teach you about God's desire for you?

13. a. What reason does Paul give for his multiple commands in the previous two verses (6:19)? What does this mean?

   b. In your experience, how much of a motivation does this usually produce in our culture? In our churches? Explain.

14. Do we often connect the way we use our money with our status in "the coming age" (6:19)? Explain.

_____

_____

_____

_____

_____

15. Why do you think Paul would spend so much time in a personal letter to his young friend, instructing him on money and its proper use? What does money have to do with the growth (or lack of it) of a local body of believers?

_____

_____

_____

_____

16. What part of Paul's teaching about money in this passage encourages you the most? What part of it surprises you the most? What part threatens you the most? Explain.

_____

_____

_____

_____

_____

_____

Optional Application:
Spend a few moments today thinking about your eternal inheritance. What kind of "reward" do you think you've built up so far? How has your use of the money God has given you either contributed to your inheritance or taken away from it? Are you satisfied with this "mid-term" evaluation? Explain.

Optional Application:
Take a month to do an analysis of your spending habits to see where your money is going. How much of your paycheck do you use on monthly bills? Giving to church or charities? Recreation? Luxury items? Debt repayment? Savings? Do you believe the Lord is happy with what you find? Why, or why not?

Optional Application:
The best way to break
money's power over us
is to give it away. Look
for a worthy charity in
your community that you
have never supported
before. Then write out a
check to support it that
actually "hurts" a bit.

17. Write any questions you have concerning Paul's
    teaching on money and its use. Discuss these ques-
    tions as a group, searching for related texts in other
    portions of Scripture.

_____

_____

_____

_____

_____

_____

_____

For the group

Money is a powerful force in our lives. It has the power
to help people and to do good, but if used unwisely,
money can cause great harm. In this passage, Paul
instructs Timothy on its proper uses.

Begin this session by asking group members
about money. How was money regarded in their fami-
lies when they were young? How has that affected how
they view money today? What do they wish they could
accomplish with it?

1 TIMOTHY 6:11-16,20-21

Final Charge

Paul had instructed Timothy about the effective workings of the church, drawing on his vast experience with churches around the Roman world. He encouraged his young friend, warned him, gave him specific commands, advised him, and admonished him. Now he ends his letter with a final charge, a last directive to be sure that Timothy follows all the instructions contained in the letter.

The charge is not harsh or demanding or authoritarian, but rather reflects Paul's great affection for Timothy as well as his deep concern for the church at Ephesus. The apostle wishes he could be with Timothy during the difficult days that he knows lie ahead—but in lieu of that, he will do his best to encourage his friend and equip him to face the challenges courageously that are certainly coming. Timothy will need such encouragement—as we do today.

Man of God (6:11). A common designation for prophets in the Old Testament (see 1 Samuel 9:6, 1 Kings 12:22). While it is unclear whether Paul means to use it as a formal title, it does seem appropriate that he would use it to refer to Timothy, a young man in God's service who represents God and who speaks in His name.

Good confession (6:12). Probably the reference is to Timothy's profession of faith in Christ at a significant time in his life, perhaps his baptism, when

For Further Study: The title "man of God" has a long and distinguished history in Scripture, so when Paul used it to describe Timothy it must have been a special encouragement. Consider the following uses of this term: Deuteronomy 33:1; Joshua 14:6; Judges 13:6; 1 Samuel 2:27; 1 Kings 12:22, 17:18; 2 Kings 4:16; Nehemiah 12:24; Jeremiah 35:4.

many witnesses were present. Compare this to what Paul says about the Lord Jesus' "good confession" in 6:13.

1. Of all the titles Paul could have chosen to refer to his young friend, why do you suppose he picked "man of God"? How would this be a special encouragement to Timothy?

_____

_____

_____

_____

2. What is Timothy commanded to avoid in 6:11?

_____

_____

_____

3. What does Paul say he should pursue instead (6:11)? List and discuss each of the six elements.

_____

_____

_____

_____

_____

_____

_____

_____

_____

4. For the second time Paul tells Timothy to "fight the good fight" of faith (6:11, see also 1:18). Why is it especially appropriate for Paul to use this image to talk with Timothy about the Christian walk?

_____

_____

_____

_____

_____

5. How can Timothy—or any of us—"take hold of eternal life" (6:12)? What exactly is Paul's admonition here?

_____

_____

_____

_____

_____

6. How is Timothy's "good confession" in 6:12 connected to Jesus' "good confession" in 6:13? In what way is any believer's "good confession" thus related to these? What is similar in each one?

_____

_____

_____

_____

_____

_____

For Thought and Discussion: When you think of the Christian life as a "fight," what comes to mind? What elements of such a "fight" can you identify? What weapons do we have to fight with? Who or what is the enemy we fight? What are we fighting for—what is our goal? What kind of strategies must we use to be victorious? Using these kinds of analogies, discuss together what it takes to win a spiritual fight.

For Thought and Discussion: How can Paul admonish Timothy to "take hold of the eternal life to which you were called" if he was saved the moment he confessed Jesus Christ as his Lord and Savior (see Romans 10)? What was left to "take hold of"? See also Colossians 1:21-23.

For Further Study: The idea of a positive "confessing" or a "confession" (as distinct from confessing sin) is a common and important biblical theme. Consider the following verses: 1 Kings 8:33-35; 2 Chronicles 6:24-26; John 1:20, 12:42; Romans 10:9-10, 14:11; Philippians 2:11; Hebrews 3:1, 13:15.

7. Why do you think Paul characterizes God as the one "who gives life to everything" in 1 Timothy 6:13? Why would this designation be especially appropriate in this context?

_____

_____

_____

_____

8. With what does Paul charge Timothy in 6:13-14? Is this anything new, or is this said for emphasis? Explain.

_____

_____

_____

_____

9. What great event is foretold in 6:14? How does Paul use this event to motivate Timothy to godliness? How can we use this same event for the same ends?

_____

_____

_____

_____

10. a. What "timing" (6:15) does Paul give for the great event described above?

_____

_____

b. How is this significant for us today?

_____

_____

_____

11. What further description does Paul give of God in 6:15-16? List the seven characteristics and discuss the significance of each.

_____

_____

_____

_____

_____

_____

_____

_____

_____

_____

For Further Study: Far from being an esoteric or impractical exercise, the study of prophecy as it is represented in Scripture is a practical discipline. Such a study reveals that the Lord's return is often used as a motivation for holy living in the here-and-now. Consider the following: John 14:1-4; Acts 17:30-31; 1 Corinthians 15:29-58; 2 Corinthians 5:1-10; 1 Thessalonians 3:11-13, 5:1-11; 2 Peter 3:7-14.

For Further Study: For centuries pseudo-scholars and "Bible students" have claimed to discover the exact date of the Lord's return. Always they have turned out to be wrong. But even this failure was predicted. Consider the following texts: Matthew 24:4-14, 23-28,36,42-44; 25:13; Acts 1:6-7.

Study Skill—Meditation

Use 1 Timothy 6:15-16 as a devotional guide in the same way that earlier in this study you may have used 1 Timothy 3:16. On each day of the week, meditate on a different aspect of God's nature, such as:

- Day One: "The blessed Ruler."
- Day Two: "The only Ruler."
- Day Three: "The King of kings."
- Day Four: "The Lord of lords."
- Day Five: "The only immortal One."
- Day Six: "The One who lives in unapproachable light."
- Day Seven: "The One whom no one has seen or can see."

Think of what each of these titles teaches you about God—what it means to you, to your family, for the future, etc. And be sure to thank God for being all of these things on your behalf.

Optional Application:
Try to break down what it means to "guard" something that has been entrusted to you. How do you effectively guard a treasure? What do you do? What don't you do? After you have thought through what it means to be a guard in general, come up with a specific plan to guard the treasure that God has entrusted to you. What do you need to do to guard this eternal treasure effectively?

For Thought and Discussion: In your opinion, why do you think it's easy for us to get sucked into "godless chatter"? What is appealing about it? And what is attractive about "the opposing ideas of what is falsely called knowledge"? Why do "secrets" like these have such power over so many of us? How can we break this power?

12. What is ascribed to God at the end of 6:16? Why do you think Paul would focus on these two items at the end of this passage?

_____

_____

_____

_____

13. a. What does Paul instruct Timothy to do at the beginning of 6:20? How is this a good summary of everything that has been written in this epistle?

_____

_____

_____

_____

   b. In what way is it another aspect of the "fight" that he has mentioned twice already?

_____

_____

_____

_____

14. What negative command does Paul give in 6:20? Where have you seen such a command given before in this letter? Do you believe such commands are necessary for today? Why, or why not?

_____

_____

_____

_____

_____

15. a. What warning is given in 6:21? How can professing a certain kind of knowledge cause one to wander from the faith?

_____

_____

_____

_____

_____

    b. Have you ever seen an example of this? If so, describe it.

_____

_____

_____

_____

_____

16. What is the significance of Paul's last sentence, "Grace be with you"? Paul surrounds his letter with grace at the beginning and end. Can you think of any reason Paul might begin his letter with grace *to* Timothy and end it with grace *with* him?

_____

_____

_____

_____

17. What questions do you have from this final portion of 1 Timothy? List them here and discuss them as a group.

_____

_____

_____

_____

_____

_____

For the group

In this passage, Paul wraps up his letter to Timothy with some final words of advice. The advice given was important to Timothy, since he knew hard times were ahead and Paul might not come to help for a while.

Begin this session by asking group members to describe the kinds of advice they've been given in their Christian walk. What advice was most helpful? Least helpful?

LOOKING BACK

By now you should have a thorough grasp of 1 Timothy and can even explain the contents of this important letter to a new believer in the faith. Yet it's also possible that you may have forgotten some of what you have studied. A review is the best way to clarify and reinforce what you have learned.

We suggest that you take a few minutes to reread 1 Timothy in its entirety and glance through the past nine lessons. A half hour of reviewing the previous lessons, rereading your completed outline (or the one on pages 13-14), and thumbing through the epistle should bring back to you the most important things you've learned. Recall from lesson 1 what you thought the book's main messages were.

Don't treat the following questions as if they were part of a comprehensive, final exam that requires deep theologizing. Instead, think of yourself explaining these things to a brand-new Christian who is unfamiliar with the church and its operation. Your goal here is to be able to explain the message of the book to ordinary people.

1. What general *concerns* did Paul express repeatedly in this epistle (see 1:3-4,6-7,18-19; 4:1-3,7; 5:7-8, 13,20,22; 6:3-5,9-10,20-21)?

   _____

   _____

   _____

_____

_____

_____

_____

_____

_____

2. What instructions did Paul give to enable the church to operate in an *orderly fashion*?

_____

_____

_____

_____

_____

3. What instructions did Paul give specifically to *Timothy*?

_____

_____

_____

_____

_____

4. What did Paul teach in this epistle about the *character* or *nature* of God and Jesus Christ?

_____

_____

_____

_____

_____

5. Briefly explain the most important points of the epistle as you understand it.

_____

_____

_____

_____

_____

_____

Optional Application:
Now that you have completed this study, perhaps something new has come to mind that you would like to concentrate on. If so, bring it before God in prayer. Write anything that you decide.

6. Have you noticed any areas (thoughts, attitudes, opinions, behavior) in which you have changed as a result of your study of 1 Timothy? If so, describe them.

_____

_____

_____

_____

_____

7. Look back over the entire study at answers to questions that express a desire to make specific personal application. Are you satisfied with your follow-through? Why, or why not? Pray about any of those areas that you think you should continue to pursue.

_____

_____

_____

_____

_____

105

Summary

One way of dealing with a major review is to get a large pad of paper or an erasable board and write on it everything the group remembers about the primary meaning of 1 Timothy. List the group's thoughts from question 1 in this lesson. After about five minutes of brainstorming, ask the group to summarize the list into a sentence or two of clear, concise definition—something everyone can remember and explain to nonChristians. Then continue to brainstorm and summarize question 2, and so on.

Be sure to save at least ten to fifteen minutes to examine how you've changed (question 6) and how you plan to continue applying what you've learned (questions 7 and 8). This is a time to encourage and motivate each other to keep going. You may not see dramatic changes in your lives yet; instead, you may see areas you want to continue praying and acting on. Remind the group that God is responsible for results; we are responsible for consistent prayer and trust.

If anyone still has questions about 1 Timothy, plan ways of finding answers. The sources beginning on page 107 may help.

Finally, evaluate how well your group functioned during your study of 1 Timothy. Some questions you might ask:

- What did you learn about small-group study?
- How well did your study help you understand 1 Timothy?
- What were the most important truths you discovered together about God?
- What did you like best about your meetings?
- What did you like least? What would you change?
- How well did you meet the goals you set at the beginning?
- What are members' current needs? What will you do next?

Now thank God for what He has taught you about yourself and His character. Thank Him for specific ways He is changing you through your study of 1 Timothy. Thank Him also for your group, and for the freedom to study the Bible together.

STUDY AIDS

For further information on the material covered in this study, consider the following sources. If your local bookstore does not have them, ask the bookstore to order them from the publishers, or find them in a public, university, or seminary library.

Commentaries on 1 Timothy

Earle, Ralph, "1,2 Timothy." *The Expositor's Bible Commentary*, Volume 11, gen. ed. Frank E. Gaebelein (Grand Rapids: Zondervan Publishing House, 1978).
A fine, verse-by-verse exposition of the message of 1 Timothy, based on the *New International Version* of the Holy Bible, presented by a conservative scholar. The whole series is marked by insightful commentary, a strong devotional concern, and extensive but not exhaustive notes from the original Greek text.

Guthrie, Donald, "The Pastoral Epistles." *The Tyndale New Testament Commentaries* (Grand Rapids: Eerdmans Pub. Co., 1957).
A straightforward, brief, helpful commentary by one of contemporary evangelicalism's leading scholars. Designed especially for lay readers rather than for academicians.

Hendriksen, William, "Exposition of the Pastoral Epistles." *New Testament Commentary* (Grand Rapids: Baker Book House, 1957).
An expository, or sermon-like, approach to verse-by-verse commentary. Very readable and inspiring. Separates analysis of the Greek from the main exposition to avoid troubling the lay person. Each section includes "Practical Lessons"—suggestions of how the passage applies today.

Kent, Homer A., Jr., *The Pastoral Epistles, Studies in I and II Timothy and Titus* (Chicago: Moody Press, 1958).

The favorite of many seminary professors, this book combines pastoral concern with a conservative viewpoint and more scholarly interests. A standard in the field for many years.

Lea, Thomas D., "1, 2 Timothy and Titus." *The New American Commentary* (Nashville: Broadman Press, 1992).
One of the more recent additions to the field. This volume (and series) covers topics somewhat more in-depth than most commentaries aimed at a pastoral audience, but is not highly technical. Tends not to break new ground so much as summarize the findings of earlier commentators, and yet is helpful for that very reason.

Historical sources

Bruce, F.F. *New Testament History* (New York: Doubleday, 1971).
A readable history of Herodian kings, Roman governors, philosophical schools, Jewish sects, Jesus, the early Jerusalem church, Paul, and early gentile Christianity. Well-documented with footnotes for the serious student, but the notes do not intrude.

Harrison, E.F. *Introduction to the New Testament* (Grand Rapids, Mich.: Eerdmans, 1971).
History from Alexander the Great—who made Greek culture dominant in the biblical world—through philosophies, pagan and Jewish religion, Jesus' ministry and teaching, and the spread of Christianity. Very good maps and photographs of the land, art, and architecture of New Testament times.

Hiebert, D. Edmond, *An Introduction to the New Testament* (Chicago: Moody Press, 1977).
A conservative, easily digested guide to the systematic interpretation of the New Testament. Books are treated in chronological order with emphasis on their eschatology, soteriology, Christology, or ecclesiology.

Concordances, dictionaries, and handbooks

A *concordance* lists words of the Bible alphabetically along with each verse in which the word appears. It lets you do your own word studies. An *exhaustive* concordance lists every word used in a given translation, while an *abridged* or *complete* concordance omits either some words, some occurrences of the word, or both.

Two of the three best exhaustive concordances are the venerable *Strong's Exhaustive Concordance* and *Young's Analytical Concordance to the Bible.* Both are available based on the *King James Version* and the *New American Standard Bible. Strong's* has an index in which you can find out which Greek or Hebrew word is used in a given English verse (although its information is occasionally outdated). *Young's* breaks up each English word it translates. Neither concordance requires knowledge of the original languages.

Perhaps the best exhaustive concordance currently on the market is *The NIV Exhaustive Concordance*. It features a Hebrew-to-English and a Greek-to-English lexicon (based on the eclectic text underlying the NIV), which are also keyed to *Strong's* numbering system.

Among other good, less expensive concordances, *Cruden's Complete Concordance* is keyed to the *King James* and *Revised Versions*, the *NIV Complete Concordance* is keyed to the *New International Version*. These include all references to every word included, but they omit "minor" words. They also lack indexes to the original languages.

A **Bible dictionary** or **Bible encyclopedia** alphabetically lists articles about people, places, doctrines, important words, customs, and geography of the Bible.

The New Bible Dictionary, edited by J.D. Douglas, F.F. Bruce, J.I. Packer, N. Hillyer, D. Guthrie, A.R. Millard, and D.J. Wiseman (Tyndale, 1982) is more comprehensive than most dictionaries. Its 1,300 pages include quantities of information along with excellent maps, charts, diagrams, and an index for cross-referencing.

Unger's Bible Dictionary by Merrill F. Unger (Moody, 1979) is equally good and is available in an inexpensive paperback edition.

The Zondervan Pictorial Encyclopedia edited by Merrill C. Tenney (Zondervan, 1975, 1976) is excellent and exhaustive, and has been revised and updated. Its five 1,000-page volumes represent a significant financial investment, however, and all but very serious students may prefer to use it at a church, public, college, or seminary library.

Unlike a Bible dictionary in the above sense, *Vine's Expository Dictionary of New Testament Words* by W.E. Vine (various publishers) alphabetically lists major words used in the *King James Version* and defines each New Testament Greek word that the KJV translates with its English word. *Vine's* also lists verse references where that Greek word appears, so you can do your own cross-references and word studies without knowing any Greek.

Vine's is a good, basic book for beginners, but it is much less complete than other Greek helps for English speakers. More serious students might prefer *The New International Dictionary of New Testament Theology*, edited by Colin Brown (Zondervan) or *The Theological Dictionary of the New Testament* by Gerhard Kittel and Gerhard Friedrich, abridged in one volume by Geoffrey W. Bromiley (Eerdmans).

A **Bible atlas** can be a great aid to understanding what is going on in a book of the Bible and how geography affected events. Here are a few good choices.

The Macmillan Atlas by Yohanan Aharoni and Michael Avi-Yonah (Macmillan, 1968, 1977) contains 264 maps, 89 photos, and 12 graphics. The many maps of individual events portray battles, movements of people, and changes of boundaries in detail.

The New Bible Atlas by J.J. Bimson and J.P. Kane (Tyndale, 1985) has 73 maps, 34 photos, and 34 graphics. Its evangelical perspective, concise and helpful text, and excellent research make it a very good choice, but its greatest strength lies in outstanding graphics, such as cross-sections of the Dead Sea.

The Bible Mapbook by Simon Jenkins (Lion, 1984) is much shorter and less expensive than most other atlases, so it offers a good first taste of the usefulness of maps. It contains 91 simple maps, very little text, and 20 graphics. Some of the graphics are computer-generated and intriguing.

The Moody Atlas of Bible Lands by Barry J. Beitzel (Moody, 1984), is scholarly, evangelical, and full of theological text, indexes, and references. This admirable reference work will be too deep and costly for some, but Beitzel shows vividly how God prepared the land of Israel perfectly for the acts of salvation He planned to accomplish in it.

A *handbook* of biblical customs can also be useful. Some good ones are *Today's Handbook of Bible Times and Customs* by William L. Coleman (Bethany, 1984) and the less detailed *Daily Life in Bible Times* (Nelson, 1982).

For Small Group Leaders

The Small Group Leader's Handbook by Steve Barker et al. (InterVarsity, 1982).
Written by an InterVarsity small group with college students primarily in mind. It includes information on small group dynamics and how to lead in light of them, and many ideas for worship, building community, and outreach. It has a good chapter on doing inductive Bible study.

Getting Together: A Guide for Good Groups by Em Griffin (InterVarsity, 1982).
Applies to all kinds of groups, not just Bible studies. From his own experience, Griffin draws deep insights into why people join groups; how people relate to each other; and principles of leadership, decision making, and discussions. It is fun to read, but its 229 pages will take more time than the above book.

You Can Start a Bible Study Group by Gladys Hunt (Harold Shaw, 1984).
Builds on Hunt's thirty years of experience leading groups. This book is wonderfully focused on God's enabling. It is both clear and applicable for Bible study groups of all kinds.

How to Build a Small Groups Ministry by Neal F. McBride (NavPress, 1994).
This hands-on workbook for pastors and lay leaders includes everything you need to know to develop a plan that fits your unique church. Through basic principles, case studies, and worksheets, McBride leads you through twelve logical steps for organizing and administering a small groups ministry.

How to Lead Small Groups by Neal F. McBride (NavPress, 1990).
Covers leadership skills for all kinds of small groups—Bible study, fellowship, task, and support groups. Filled with step-by-step guidance and practical exercises to help you grasp the critical aspects of small group leadership and dynamics.

DJ Plus, a special section in *Discipleship Journal* (NavPress, bimonthly).
Unique. Three pages of this feature are packed with practical ideas for small groups. Writers discuss what they are currently doing as small group members and leaders. To subscribe, write to Subscription Services, Post Office Box 54470, Boulder, Colorado 80323-4470.

Bible study methods

Braga, James. *How to Study the Bible* (Multnomah, 1982).
   Clear chapters on a variety of approaches to Bible study: synthetic, geographical, cultural, historical, doctrinal, practical, and so on. Designed to help the ordinary person without seminary training to use these approaches.

Fee, Gordon, and Douglas Stuart. *How to Read the Bible for All Its Worth* (Zondervan, 1982).
   After explaining in general what interpretation and application are, Fee and Stuart offer chapters on interpreting and applying the different kinds of writing in the Bible: Epistles, Gospels, Old Testament Law, Old Testament narrative, the Prophets, Psalms, Wisdom, and Revelation. Fee and Stuart also suggest good commentaries on each biblical book. They write as evangelical scholars who personally recognize Scripture as God's Word for their daily lives.

Jensen, Irving L. *Independent Bible Study* (Moody, 1963), and *Enjoy Your Bible* (Moody, 1962).
   The former is a comprehensive introduction to the inductive Bible study method, especially the use of synthetic charts. The latter is a simpler introduction to the subject.

Wald, Oletta. *The Joy of Discovery in Bible Study* (Augsburg, 1975).
   Wald focuses on issues such as how to observe all that is in a text, how to ask questions of a text, how to use grammar and passage structure to see the writer's point, and so on. Very helpful on these subjects.

Titles in the LifeChange series:

Genesis	2 Corinthians
Exodus	Galatians
Joshua	Ephesians
Ruth & Esther	Philippians
1 Samuel	Colossians/Philemon
Proverbs	1 Thessalonians
Isaiah	1 Timothy
Mark	Titus
Luke	Hebrews
John	James
Acts	1 Peter
Romans	1, 2, & 3 John
1 Corinthians	Revelation

SMALL-GROUP MATERIALS FROM NAVPRESS

BIBLE STUDY SERIES

DESIGN FOR DISCIPLESHIP
GOD IN YOU
GOD'S DESIGN FOR THE FAMILY
INSTITUTE OF BIBLICAL
   COUNSELING Series
LEARNING TO LOVE Series

LIFECHANGE
RADICAL RELATIONSHIPS
SPIRITUAL DISCIPLINES
STUDIES IN CHRISTIAN LIVING
THINKING THROUGH DISCIPLESHIP

TOPICAL BIBLE STUDIES

Becoming a Woman of Excellence
Becoming a Woman of Freedom
Becoming a Woman of Prayer
Becoming a Woman of Purpose
The Blessing Study Guide
Homemaking
Intimacy with God
Loving Your Husband

Loving Your Wife
A Mother's Legacy
Praying From God's Heart
Surviving Life in the Fast Lane
To Run and Not Grow Tired
To Walk and Not Grow Weary
What God Does When Men Pray
When the Squeeze Is On

BIBLE STUDIES WITH COMPANION BOOKS

Bold Love
Daughters of Eve
The Discipline of Grace
The Feminine Journey
Inside Out
The Masculine Journey
The Practice of Godliness
The Pursuit of Holiness

Secret Longings of the Heart
Spiritual Disciplines
Tame Your Fears
Transforming Grace
Trusting God
What Makes a Man?
The Wounded Heart

RESOURCES

Brothers!
Discipleship Journal's 101 Best
   Small-Group Ideas
How to Build a Small-Groups Ministry
How to Lead Small Groups
Jesus Cares for Women
The Navigator Bible Studies
   Handbook

The Small Group Leaders
   Training Course
Topical Memory System
   (KJV/NIV and NASB/NKJV)
Topical Memory System:
   Life Issues